THE MYTHS OF OUR FOUNDING FATHERS
AND THEIR CONSTITUTION

THE TRUTHS WE NEED TO KNOW FOR THE 21ST CENTURY

THE MYTHS OF OUR

FOUNDING FATHERS

AND THEIR

CONSTITUTION

THE TRUTHS WE NEED TO KNOW FOR THE 21ST CENTURY

By
Randy Bell

Published by
McKee Learning Foundation

ISBN-13:   978-0-9895428-3-8

Published by
        McKee Learning Foundation

For more information, contact:

        Info@McKeeLearningFoundation.com

        www.McKeeLearningFoundation.com

TABLE OF CONTENTS

APPENDICES

DEDICATION

"A knowledge of history and tradition of one's locality

is not essential to the production of a livelihood,

but to know and respect one's forebears and

their contributions to the progress

of our civilization and culture

is a worthwhile accomplishment.

(anonymous)

I. PREFACE

In our political debates today, we all too often hear intoned that "the Founding Fathers believed (this and that)" offered up to lend credibility to the speaker's argument. Similarly, we hear that "the Constitution specifies (thus and so)." The rhetorical assumption is that an opponent's proposals are wholly contrary to what our hallowed Founding Fathers believed and set out to accomplish, as reflected in the specificity and clarity of our Constitution. The arguments of the speaker are presumed to be grounded in that same sacred purity of the Founders and their Constitution. Thereby, any disagreement with such sanctity is unacceptable – if not outright treasonable.

All of these perceptions are, of course, hogwash. Whenever a speaker intones such lofty historical blessing upon his/her political (and parochial) agenda, most often they instead demonstrate a complete lack of understanding about the reality of our Founders and the Constitutional form of government they created. Such false arguments often beg us to question whether our political leaders have any idea what the true story of our American History really is. Particularly as regards the history of those individuals who led the founding of this country, and what is embedded in their unique Constitution and the radically new form of government that it established. How it all came about in little over a decade remains one of humankind's fascinating stories and great accomplishments.

Perhaps inevitably, the American people have tended to deify those all-too-human beings who created the physical and intellectual foundation of this country. We think of them as unquestionable, infallible, and of one elective and unified mind, of common vision,

1

with a unanimously shared outcome. Nothing could be further from the truth of those times.

Understanding the diversity of thought, the balancing of interests, and the fragility of the Revolutionary and Constitutional founding of this Republic, is the Purpose of this book. It is to strip away the lazy argument of the politician who seeks the divine blessing of the Founders to support a questionable position. It is to enable us to reflect on the real intentions and human struggles of those Founders, and how they overcame their divisions to create a new whole. From this better understanding, we can more properly draw guidance from them in surmounting our own modern-day divisions.

The work of our nation's Founders, and their Constitution that embodies that work, deserves our attention and respect. Not our deification. Not forcing these individual Founders into one blurred, amalgamated whole. Not rewriting their history to suit our own purposes. Rather, the scope of participants in this founding, their individuality, the difficult issues to be resolved resulting from their differences, and the corresponding divisions across the new nation that came perilously close to wrecking the whole effort, is our Focus.

II. INTRODUCTION

"The cause of America is in a great measure the cause of all
mankind."[1]
(Thomas Paine, *Common Sense*, 1776)

On a quiet day in late April, 1607, three English sailing ships
slipped cautiously into a bay bordered by something mostly unseen
by them for months – land. The ships had left London in late
December, and now at long last they had reached their intended
target: "Virginia." New lands in the New World, here for the
riches and benefit of England and all those who would follow to
this new continent.

As the 101 men and boys stood on the decks of their three ships –
the aptly named Susan Constant, Discovery, and Godspeed – one
can only imagine their thoughts. Thoughts of gold, certainly, since
that was what their English sponsors had charged them with
finding. Feelings of excitement, because there could be no
denying the thrill of a new and unique adventure. Feelings of
relief, having survived the long sailing to arrive here. Can we also
imagine perhaps their thoughts of "why am I here, on this deck, at
this step-off stop, for what greater purpose?" Was there any hint
that this little party of adventurers and settlers was in fact part of
something of far larger significance? Any sense that they were
merely the opening sentence of a great novel ready to be written?
Or conversely, that they were the last chapter of an old novel
nearing its completion?

On April 26, a small group of the adventurers made a tentative
landing on the tip of the southern cape of what would later be

called Chesapeake Bay. Chaplain Robert Hunt said a short prayer with that first group assembled:

> "Almighty God … we beseech Thee to bless us and this plantation which we and our nation have begun in Thy fear and Thy glory … Lord, sanctify our spirits and give us holy hearts, that so we may be Thy instruments in this most glorious work."[2]

The adventurers would have a few weeks to look, to ponder, to imagine the sights seen from those decks. But on May 14, 1607, the full contingent departed their ships onto an island which they called Jamestown in honor of their King. On that day, the English settlement of America was permanently begun, and America's chapter of civilization's story began to be written.

America is a continuous work in process. Never stationary, always moving towards something new, a something only vaguely known. It is a drama not fully scripted, a promise not yet kept, a goal not yet achieved, an accomplishment not yet satisfactory. It is filled with restless people always struggling for something "better." America has constantly been a living dream, working its way towards becoming a complete reality, moving incrementally a generation at a time as that dream is passed on to our children.

Turning that dream into a reality would require a number of successive major steps, carried out over nearly two centuries. Steps that would proceed incrementally, most often by the seat of their collective pants, without a clear view of the destination target. First would come the people, a growing population of settlers from across most all of Old Europe to full this new, vast, raw and unexplored land. The people had widely differing motivations for coming here, but all sailed on a ship called "opportunity." The opportunity for a fresh start, a better life, a life of their own making, than existed for them and their children in the rigged and rigid caste system of Europe's kings and inherited rights of birth.

Coming out of their migratory experiences; settling in an unfamiliar, undeveloped place; having individual responsibility to live so as to survive: all of these things served to form a collective character and culture appropriate to this brand-new civilization. The "American Character" took root, and it was a vastly different character of opportunity, self-reliance within community, and individual freedom and equality than had ever been seen in Europe.

With a stable and distributed population achieved over the first 168 years, with a different mindset from their fellow citizens back in Europe, it then remained for Colonial America to take the next three critical steps in order to go its own destined way by founding a separate nation: 1) Independence, gained through winning a war of Revolution; 2) Unification, achieved by establishing a first National Congress under the Articles of Confederation; and 3) Governance, created under a written Constitution of structure and rules, in a radically new form here-to-fore unknown to the human species. From these three steps, "Colonial America" as an extension of England and its King would become the free and independent "United States of America" under the will of The People. Three steps, over 13 years from 1775-1788, led by otherwise ordinary people doing extraordinary things at great risk to themselves. The people we call America's "Founding Fathers."

Yet we are not even in agreement as to who constitutes the Founding Fathers. Some might well argue that all of the brave colonists who came to and settled this country warrant being called our Founding Fathers and Mothers. They created a unique civilization and supporting infrastructure where nothing already existed in place. They populated that civilization with people of widely different cultures, backgrounds, wealth (or lack thereof), and religious faiths. They assimilated this diversity into something called an "American" without resort to war and violence as had so often been the case back in their European home countries. That rank and file population created the country of America, and at a certain needed moment in time broke it free into an independent one, free to exercise its choices for its own destiny – choices that could have taken it into many different directions.

But it fell to a smaller group of persons to unite thirteen highly independent and self-minded colonies into one "United States of America." A group able to convince the population of this new country to give up some of their newly-won independence, and give themselves over to one shared, larger whole. Critical to making that choice was for that group to act wisely on their behalf, provide leadership when needed, and to devise a wholly new model of government never seen before that would balance needs for common action with the freedom to go one's own way. A government run by the People, not a select group of hereditary royals.

So the People created the <u>country</u>; the Founding Fathers created the <u>unified nation and its government</u>. 118 men who, from 1775 to 1788, in differing combinations of time and service: wrote a *Declaration of Independence*; accepted an initial *Articles of Confederation and Perpetual Union* (such union to be called "The United States of America"); accepted that that Confederation form of government was inadequate and needed to be replaced; and then devised the remarkable *Constitution of the United States* – a constitution adopted by the people by the most narrow of margins. It is to these Founding Fathers to which we give our attention.

We all know a few familiar names that we typically call forth – Washington, Jefferson, Franklin, Adams – but how far down the roll call of Founders do we go? These were all white men, but of a wide range of age and financial standing. For the most part previously unknown to each other, they came together across the wide and differing geographies and economies of Colonial America, from New Hampshire in the north to Georgia in the south. They shared traits of good intelligence and dedication to

6

service to their home colony/state. But such traits and their personal experiences led them to very different, yet deeply held, spiritual, economic, social, and political beliefs.

These strong and differing beliefs time and time again threatened to derail the whole founding enterprise: the establishment of this one nation, these United States of America. It was an idea, an ideal, that just barely made it to fruition. That it ultimately did reflected a trust in each other, a willingness to give a little to get a lot, and a continuous focus on achieving a greater good and fulfilling an inspired Purpose that transcended partisan divides and individual prerogatives.

It is those people, their times, the pressing difficult issues that divided them, and the surmounting of those divisions that is instructive for us today. It is this story we tell in this narrative.

"The brotherhood of man may be a noble ideal,
but can it be achieved in any society that is not homogeneous?"[3]
(Vine Deloria, Jr., Native-American writer)

III. COMING TOGETHER

It was a sunny day in Philadelphia on May 10, 1775. Springtime is designed to uplift our spirit, infuse us with a sense of new optimism and renewal, give us energy for the work to be done in the seasons that follow. But this sun would only temporarily disguise the dark clouds moving over the land. In the thirteen English colonies that had been established on the Atlantic coastline of the vast area called "America," a movement was afoot. A movement first of resistance to the old order, then a movement of separation, to be followed by a wholly new union. A transformation from being colonies of the old European order with its 1000-year history of rules and structure, into a new order without precedent. In Philadelphia that day, over 50 men were gathering who would come to lead the beginning of that movement, one gradual step at a time, moving irrevocably forward. Ever mindful of, and guided by, the brief history of this thing they called "America."

For almost two centuries, adventurers in America had focused on the act of colonizing this vast, unknown and untamed land. Lands harder and more primitive than these colonists had left behind, but rich with natural resources open to all. Thus the people had the expectation of ultimately achieving far more than they had ever before known. The first permanent colony had been established at Jamestown, Virginia, in 1607 – almost 168 years to the day before this sunny day of gathering in 1775 Philadelphia – seeking economic opportunities and rewards. The second colony would be at Plimouth, Massachusetts in 1620, established by Puritan refugees seeking relief from religious persecution in England. Each of these colonies exemplified the fundamental – and often conflicting – basis for the movement to America: economic opportunity and religious freedom. Unfortunately, both would subsequently also exemplify that these would not necessarily be open to all. Virginia would become the colony of a new wealthy class of large estates supported by African slaves, dominating the individual small farmer. Massachusetts would become as repressive to other religious faiths as they had previously been so oppressed.

So it would be left to others to provide for a middle ground of economic, religious and legal freedom in the eleven other colonies that followed. And that meant opening the door not just to English colonists, but to potential colonists from all of the British Isles and Western Europe. They came slowly at first, but the trickle turned into a flood. All drawn by the opportunity to achieve based upon one's own initiatives and hard work, rather than the royal caste system of Europe that limited one's opportunities based upon birth. Even if such opportunity could not be realized in one's own lifetime, these colonists believed that life for their children would always be better with their descendants. This would be the American Dream, and it would be a dream handed down through each generation. "Opportunity" would be the true American inheritance, available to everyone.

Settling the American wilderness had been the priority for 168 years. But it had worked, and the thirteen colonies were thriving domestically and in foreign trade. From the small towns and tradespeople of the northern colonies, to the rural countryside of the "food basket" of southern agriculture, to the dense wilderness forests of the western borders, the population was growing. They had built quite a something out of quite the nothing that they had encountered, all through their own hard work, decision-making, and personal sacrifice. Some of it had been done literally single-handedly, some by working together in small communities; individuality and community were always a delicate balance. And as long as the colonies were profitable and caused no trouble, England and its kings – thousands of miles away across the expansive ocean, with no understanding of what life in America was truly like – fortuitously left them alone to develop and manage on their own.

But as with any family, at some point the child grows up and gets restless. Itching to be on his/her own. To move out of the parents' house and live one's own life. And so had begun such colonial adolescence through the decade of 1765-1775. England's need for more cash to fund its royal wars and lifestyle would be the scratching that inflamed that itch. No longer content with the indirect wealth coming from its England/American trade, taxing the colonies directly became England's new economic plan, as decided by Parliament with no input from the colonies themselves. To the great majority of colonists accustomed to making their own decisions and already working under their own forms of local self-government, such arbitrary actions directly affecting their pocketbooks were intolerable – even if England was "the Mother Country" and their primary trading partner and benefactor.

THE COLONIAL CONGRESSES

In the 17th century, there had been a few gatherings of multiple colonies to discuss common defense strategies, principally regarding the French and the American Indians. The most significant had been the Albany Congress of 1754, attended by representatives from the seven northern colonies. Besides discussing defense strategies, it was the first formal collective meeting to also discuss creating a union of the colonies under a "Grand Council" – a formal colonial structure, with limited authority to regulate relations with the Indians and settle inter-colonial land disputes, sanctioned by, not independent of, England. The proposed structure was rejected or ignored by the various colonial legislatures eager to protect their own superior authority.

The names of the 21 representatives to this Albany Congress have long since faded into the footnotes of historical archives. With one notable exception of a 49-year-old author, newspaper publisher, scientist/inventor, and recently-elected representative to the Pennsylvania Assembly by the name of Benjamin Franklin. The proposed Grand Council was his idea, and his role in this Albany Congress served as the beginning of the long arc of his career role as the foremost guiding spirit in America's founding.

But in 1765 after the close of the French and Indian War, when England began to levy taxes directly on the colonies, tensions began to rise. The tax issue was increasingly galvanizing several of the colonies to meet to share ideas for how to respond, and how to do so collectively. (This was altogether remarkable in itself given that communication and contact among the colonists had been virtually non-existent up to that point.) Following the precedent of the Albany Congress, the Stamp Act Congress met in October 1765 in response to a call from the Massachusetts Assembly. 27 Representatives from nine colonies attended. The motivating issue was the passage by Parliament of a tax in the form of a purchased stamp to be affixed to all paper goods used in the colonies. The Stamp Act Congress produced a document entitled the "Declaration of Rights and Grievances" that declared, among other protestations, that Parliament had had no right to pass such a tax given that no representative of the colonies sat in that body. Therefore the tax was illegal and hence void. Parliament unsurprisingly rejected the Declaration, going even further to formally declare that it had the authority to legislate for the colonies "in all cases whatsoever."

The Stamp Act Congress lost the legal argument, though Parliament ultimately repealed the tax at the behest of English merchants hurt by the loss of sales from protesting colonists. (The income/trade argument was advocated to the Parliament by the aforesaid Benjamin Franklin on behalf of several of the colonies.) But the Stamp Act Congress did act as the first formally-organized and joint protest against England's rule (although the idea of independence itself was never on the table for consideration). This Congress thereby set the stage of protest, and began to bring forth some of the players, for more serious actions to come almost a decade later with the First Continental Congress of 1774. And for what would come thereafter.

THE FIRST CONTINENTAL CONGRESS

The Stamp Act Congress and the repeal of the tax by England did not prove to resolve the tax issue long-term. With outrage growing at England's continuing actions and interference, escalation of tensions and tit-for-tat responses steadily grew. Small outbreaks of non-violent and/or civil disobedient acts of protest escalated into more open resistance and vandalism. As these incidents grew, England responded in kind by sending soldiers to America not to defend the colonists, but to defend royal interest *against* those colonists. Many of these protesting acts subsequently wove themselves into our historical folklore, including the Boston Tea Party raid protesting the high tax on tea, and the shooting of five civilians by British troops on the Boston Common ("The Boston Massacre"). Protests escalated as royal governors were driven out, or tarred and feathered, as they tried to collect the taxes due on notarizing stamps which were applied to most all legal or financial transactions. Boycotts of English goods were called to protest high tariffs, and blockade runners snuck out American goods in protest of English trading restrictions

Massachusetts was the hotbed center of open protests, causing more and more British troops to be sent there to "keep the peace" (i.e. to keep the disorderly colonist protesters in check). But colonists up and down the coastline worked their own forms of resistance. Pennsylvania, Virginia, and South Carolina were also notable in their agitation. There were also voices everywhere calling for compromise, unwilling to break with England, not wanting to see harsher punishments coming down on them. But talk of open rebellion was growing stronger each day, and appeals to the English King or Parliament went lacking for an accommodating response.

So what did the colonists finally do? They did what we now always do in a crisis. The colonists rose to the occasion and formed a committee! Following the Boston Massacre and the imposition of the British blockade of Boston Harbor, calls went out to each colony for their legislatures to send representatives to a new 13-colony assembly. The first meeting of the "First Continental Congress" began on September 5, 1774. *This assemblage marked the first gathering, and the first national entity, participated in together by all of the colonies.* It had no written mandate or rules to follow or formal structure; those things would actually not come until seven years later. It was essentially an ad hoc group, empowered only to talk with each other to find any consensus and agreements possible on behalf of their respective colonies. The 13 individual colonies were still supreme; this Congress only had moral and persuasive authority acting through the individual delegates. So they agreed to write a joint letter to the King, expressing their protest and opposition to his actions, and then adjourned to wait and see what the response would be. It was not an overly auspicious beginning of a new national government for a country not yet formed, but it did establish the needed precedent. As well, it presciently resolved that, if the King disregarded their protest, a second meeting of the group would automatically be called to reassess the situation.

Fortunately for our fate as a country, King George III responded as destiny required. He dismissed the Congress's letter outright and would not even see their representative who brought the petition. Instead, he declared the colonies in "open rebellion," and warned that they needed to be brought into full subjugation to his edicts.

The majority of the English Parliament agreed fully with his stance. The door to compromise was now closed.

So the inevitable happened. In the early morning darkness of April 19, 1775, English soldiers marched out of Boston – now under military rule given its continual trouble-making – and headed northwest to destroy weapons and munitions stored in the villages outside the city. Paul Revere and William Dawes rode into history that night, alerting all the villagers and farmers on the march's path. As dawn broke over the Town Commons in Lexington, Massachusetts, a band of pulled-together riflemen with their muskets stood in the face of the English Army, the face of mighty England and its King. Who shot first is still debated; but that first shot was indeed figuratively to be "a shot heard 'round the world" over the next centuries. What was actually heard was a birth cry, an infant wail announcing that a new form of government, and a new form of nation, was getting ready to come forth on the world's stage. It would prove to be an elongated birthing, with 13 siblings needing to come together, requiring a multitude of mid-husbands and mid-wives to do the work necessary to bring this child to a safe beginning. Much work, pain, suffering, blood, intellect, will, perseverance and compromise would ultimately be required to bring this child out of the birthing room and into the nursery.

We sometimes forget that the colonists lost that battle of Lexington. Outmatched in that moment, these first fighters nevertheless bought time for more fighters to come together further down the marching path. It was at Concord that a second battle was fought that day, where the unorganized frontiersmen used the frontier itself as their strategy, as their armament. They fought as the trained frontier hunters that they were, not as professional soldiers following European "rules of engagement" that they were not. And they fought on their own grounds to defend their homes and way of life; defending one's home turf always generates several additional bonus points, as many subsequent wars and revolutions since across the globe have proven.

The American colonies were now in open rebellion against England, confirming King George's provocation towards them. It was a rebellion that many colonists believed could not be won. While many voices rang out urging to expand the fight that had now begun in Massachusetts, others continued to urge caution, to make additional entreaties to England to avoid war. But Americans had just slapped the face of the greatest world power existing. *NOW WHAT?*

IV. THE SECOND CONTINENTAL CONGRESS

CONSENSUS FOR INDEPENDENCE

And so it was that, following the Lexington and Concord showdown, the colonial delegates convened in Philadelphia in 1775 as the "Second Continental Congress." Events were now beginning to move more quickly. More entreaties were agreed to be sent to England on behalf of those who still sought to avoid war. But on June 17, 1775, the battle of Bunker Hill was fought in Charleston, next to Boston. The battle was similar to the Lexington and Concord story: around 3000 British climbed up Breed's Hill to attack the 1200 assembled colonists who had built earthworks on the high ground. At the end of the day, the colonists were routed, but with minimal losses; the British suffered 800 wounded and 226 killed – one-third of their number. This was no small skirmish, but major forces on both sides in pitched battle. And while the colonists lost the ground, they won the moral victory. They had shown that they could commendably stand and face the world-renown English army The British command structure gained a different appreciation for what would be required to defeat the colonials, requiring far more weaponry and manpower than originally believed. On the other side, King George's position against the colonists hardened; now he was committed to defeat the colonists outright. In turn, many colonists who had been seeking peace moved over to the independence side – the majority of American public opinion was irrevocably turning towards revolution.

Given England's intransigence and the outcome of Bunker Hill, the Second Continental Congress now moved to a more decisive role.

The immediate issue on its table was the need to organize for a common defense against a militarily superior and immediate enemy. They therefore authorized that the first Continental-wide army be created. It was a new <u>national standing army</u> alongside state and local militia units, to be led by their colleague in the Congress, Virginian George Washington – whose only military experience was his limited service in the French and Indian War. Whatever his military shortcomings, Washington would ultimately prove to be the uniquely inspired choice for American leadership. Washington not only innately understood the challenge of what he was about to undertake, but also its significance. In 1776, he said that, "The fate of unborn millions will now depend, under God, on the courage and conduct of this army."[1] Washington would leave the Congress and take command of the military side of America's founding o July 3, 1775, and would not be a part of the ensuing governing of the nascent country. That job would fall to the remaining delegates.

Very importantly, creating a national standing army served as a recognition that there were some needs and issues that *transcended the supremacy of the individual colonies*, where success demanded concerted action on behalf of them all. Britain's march on Lexington and Concord had done what the colonists themselves had not achieved before: beginning the unifying of themselves into a larger whole beyond just the individual, town or colony. They were not a "nation" yet, but the door had been opened and they had begun to walk, however tentatively, through it.

It should be kept in mind that the Revolutionary War was never a universally popular idea. <u>It has been variously estimated that no more than 50% of the colonists supported disengagement from England</u>. Many colonists felt that war against such a superpower was unwinnable; they feared retribution from the King; accumulated economic fortunes were at risk; social status was often linked to English backgrounds and connections; many family ties transcended the ocean between the two countries and remained vital aspects of one's sense of family. Divided loyalties could be found within extended families, neighbors, or in geographical pockets; difficult personal stories abounded.

In the face of such divided loyalties, directions were hesitant, confused. Answering that confusion, that lack of full resolve, fell to Thomas Paine. Paine was a recent immigrant to America from England, with a total disdain and outright hostility to all things royal in England. He had settled in Philadelphia and was introduced by Benjamin Franklin to the leading thinkers, debaters and politicians of the day located there. As the colonists watched the events unfolding in/around Boston and hotly debated their meanings, Paine published his pamphlet *Common Sense* in January 1776. It contained a scathing indictment of the King and English Parliament, and laid out a "common sense" reasoning for why America's separation was both required and inevitable. But over and above the logic of separation, Paine ennobled the revolutionary cause with a providential destiny from God: America was to be an example for the benefit of all nations, a first for others to follow. What the colonists were attempting was, in Paine's arguments, what should be happening the world over – throwing out monarchies in favor of equality and freedom for the common person. His writings were intended to promote both the divine intention and the earthly fulfillment of the American cause.

So he wrote:

> "*The sun never shined on a cause of greater worth.*
> 'Tis not the affair of a City, a County, a Province, or a Kingdom; but of a Continent – of at least one eighth part of the globe. 'Tis not the concern of a day, a year, or an age; posterity are virtually involved in the contest, and will be more or less affected even to the end of time, by the proceedings now. Now is the seed-time of Continental union, faith and honour."[2]

And:

> "It may not always happen that our soldiers are citizens, and the multitude [of Americans] a body of reasonable men; virtue, as I have already remarked, is not hereditary, neither is it perpetual. Should an independancy be brought about by [the legal voice of the people in Congress], we have every opportunity and every encouragement before us, to form the noblest, purest constitution on the face of the earth. We have it in our power to begin the world over again. A situation, similar to the present, hath not happened since the days of Noah until now. The birth-day of a new world is at hand, and a race of men perhaps as numerous as all Europe contains, as to receive their portion of freedom from the event of a few months. How trifling, how ridiculous, do the little, paltry cavellings, of a few weak or interested men appear, when weighed against the business of a world."[3]

And then Paine proceeded to his main point, laying out logical arguments one after another in the common language of his time as to why monarchies were inherently bad concepts, artificial modes of government against the very laws of nature, creation, and human aspirations. His premise was that a single individual needs no government at all, and can survive quite well by him-/herself – up to a point. When several persons come together, there can be multiple benefits greater than the sum of each person's individual efforts, so "society" is created by this mutual need of each other. However, given that people "are imperfect and not without vices," conflicts will arise, thereby limiting the positive benefits of a new society. Therefore, "they will begin to relax in their duty and attachment to each other: and this remissness will point out the necessity of establishing some form of government to supply the

19

defect of moral virtue."[4]   This human evolution simply reflected Paine's truth that "Society is produced by our wants, and government by our wickedness; the former promotes our happiness *positively* by uniting our affections, the latter *negatively* by restraining our vices."[5]

It was all a reasoned argument for a "bottom up" approach to government. That government existed not for kingly pleasure but only to serve the <u>collective needs determined by society itself</u>. From this posture, Paine proceeded to pillory the English King and his whole monarchical system, with its top-down hereditary basis, as being inherently against the laws of nature and humankind. After many pages supporting his indictment not just against King George III ("the Royal Brute of Britain"!) but against the whole concept of hereditary monarchical rule, there could be only one conclusion: separation. England could elect to keep their king: that was their own choice. But the American colonies had different priorities to achieve, different directions to go. And so Paine called for all colonists to come together, as such a course could not be denied:

> "WHEREFORE, instead of gazing at each other with suspicious or doubtful curiosity, let each of us, hold out to his neighbour the hearty hand of friendship, and unite in drawing a line, which, like an act of oblivion, shall bury in forgetfulness every former dissention. Let the names of Whig and Tory be extinct; and let none other be heard among us, than those of *a good citizen, an open and resolute friend, and a virtuous supporter of the* RIGHTS *of* MANKIND *and the* FREE AND INDEPENDANT STATES OF AMERICA."[6]

Words are powerful instruments, still to this day. Thomas Paine's *Common Sense* sold extremely rapidly, with an estimate of over 150,000 copies sold in Colonial America alone (perhaps one-quarter of the reading Americans at that time). It was also reprinted in several European editions. It was a strong voice at a time when strong directions and decisions were needed. That voice was heard clearly only six months later when the Second Continental Congress finally found the consensus needed.

Others better known to us today may have come together to make their unequaled Declaration of Independence. But it was Thomas Paine who rationalized the Cause and helped to prepare the way for its acceptance by sufficient numbers of the colonists. The poet had reached out and touched the heart of his audience and pleaded its case; the Continental Congress subsequently gave that heart form and legitimacy, and committed the population to its destiny.

Over the years, Paine's case-building for independence was acknowledged by his well-known contemporaries. Washington assessed Paine's impact on the Revolutionary cause by saying, "A few more of such flaming arguments, as were exhibited at Falmouth and Norfolk, added to the sound doctrine and unanswerable reasoning contained in the pamphlet Common Sense, will not leave numbers at a loss to decide upon the propriety of a separation [from England]."[7] And John Adams simply summed it up by saying, "History is to ascribe the American Revolution to Thomas Paine."[8] (John Adams)

MOVING TOWARD POLITICAL UNION

While Washington directed the Revolution on the battlefront, the 2nd Continental Congress called into session on May 10, 1775, was the organizational and intellectual side of the Revolution. It had been called into being in response to the King's total refusal to consider the colonists' demands for redress of their complaints. Among those that convened were the giants of our founding history: principally Benjamin Franklin, Thomas Jefferson, John

21

Adams, Samuel Adams, John Hancock, Roger Sherman, plus 51 others whose names we rarely can recall (see Appendix 1). Most – but not all – were fairly wealthy men, especially the delegates from the south and middle colonies, able to therefore contribute their personal time and expense money to serving in the Congress. (Indeed, many contributed their own funds to the cause when the colonial legislatures refused to ante up what was needed to continue the revolutionary fight. Yet some friends had to chip in to buy Samuel Adams [MA], who lived perpetually in debt, some new clothes during his days in Congress.) George Taylor (PA) had come to America from Ireland as an indentured servant, ultimately taking over an ironworks factory and becoming a successful businessman. In total, eight signers for independence were born outside of the American colonies.

All of the delegates were well-educated – some by their own self-learning, others by access to formal schooling. Some were great and fiery orators; others good and reasoned thinkers; others served as quiet background figures. They varied in age from the young Edward Rutledge (SC) at age 26 to Benjamin Franklin (PA) the elder statesman at 70; Thomas Jefferson (VA), the principal author of the Declaration of Independence, was only 33. They were primarily lawyers, merchants, farmer/planters, but many had worked in a variety of multiple professions during the course of their lives. Yet all were well-known public servants and respected political leaders within their own colony, had differing views about how to resolve the relationship with England, and each reserved the right to make up his own mind as to which future direction the colonies should pursue.

Separation was their primary topic for consideration from the first moment they convened. But opinions on the future course differed greatly across the colonies, with particularly strong English Loyalists in the middle colonies of New York, Pennsylvania, Delaware and New Jersey. Those differences were likewise reflected in these men and their initial conversations. Each colony was represented in the Congress, with as many individuals in each delegation as the colonial legislature chose to select. (Rhode Island ended up with two signers for independence; Pennsylvania had nine! Some delegates came and went and were replaced; some attended just some of the sessions; a few were even appointed after the Declaration was adopted but nevertheless signed it on behalf of their colony.) But each colony only had one Congressional vote, therefore each delegation had to first reach its own internal consensus by majority vote before the Congress as a whole could decide anything – all of which led to extensive and intensive deal-making and negotiating throughout the Congress' deliberations.

The ultimate decision to revolt against England came only after a long year of internal debate and political negotiation within the Congress. Some members were very reluctant to act without specific directives from their respective colonial legislature (e.g. New York – whose dithering on decisions frustrated most other delegates – and Delaware); others felt no such restrictions and were fully emboldened by their individual opinions (e.g. Virginia and Massachusetts). *It was two differing political theories of "representation" – serving as a collective surrogate of the people or elected for one's personal judgment – that continue to be debated today.* New Jersey's delegation was replaced wholesale when pro-revolutionaries who had taken control of the legislature felt that the current delegation was too pro-England.

Finally, unstoppable events and gathering momentum happening across the colonies overwhelmed their deliberations. The battles of Lexington and Concord a year before had brought the inevitability of military fighting into reality. Public opinion, influenced by the writings of Paine and the inflammatory speeches of others, had built to a sufficient mass that demanded a response from the Congress. New Hampshire had already voted to establish its own separate independence, and was in the process of establishing self-governance for their new "nation." A colonial force outside Boston had held its own against the mighty British at Bunker Hill before finally retreating, and another colonial force had decisively defeated an attempted invasion of Charleston, South Carolina by a fleet of British warships.

By July 1776, the winds of revolution across the colonies would not be abated; the passion of the oratory and logic of the arguments in the Congress would not be cooled. So on June 7, 1776, Richard Henry Lee (VA) finally called the question to end the seemingly endless debate. He introduced his resolution for independence – quickly seconded by John Adams (MA) – that said:

> *Resolved, that these United Colonies are, and by right ought to be, free and independent States; that they are absolved from all allegiance to the British Crown, and that all political connections between them and State of Great Britain is, and ought to be, totally dissolved.*

The Resolution passed.

But in this legalistic setting of a Congress, a simple motion to dissolve was not seen as enough. Looking back to England's Glorious Revolution and its Bill of Rights of 1689, the precedence of a reasoned statement of cause to justify this break with England was seen as a necessary legal element of the Colonists' revolution. A "Committee of Five" consisting of Benjamin Franklin (PA), Thomas Jefferson (VA), John Adams (MA), Roger Sherman (CT) and Robert Livingston (NY) was charged with drafting a formal statement of independence.

With Thomas Jefferson (principally), John Adams and Benjamin Franklin taking the lead in drafting this statement, Congress was moved to unanimously declare its **Declaration of Independence** from England, saying that:

"When in the course of human events it becomes necessary for one people to dissolve the political bands which have connected them with another and to assume among the powers of the earth, the separate and equal station to which the Laws of Nature and Nature's God entitle them ... We hold these truths to be self-evident, that all men are created equal, that they are endowed by their Creator with certain unalienable Rights, that among these are Life, Liberty and the pursuit of Happiness. That to secure these rights, Governments are instituted among Men, deriving their just powers from the consent of the governed ..."

On July 2nd, the Congress voted to declare its independence; on July 4th the final wording of the Declaration of Independence was approved and sent out for printing and distribution. *It was not a unanimous vote by the individual delegates within their delegations*, though in the final tally of the colonies unanimity was ultimately achieved. Some delegates hoped for more time for negotiations with England, but voted "yes" anyway after they saw which way the final tally was heading. Caesar Rodney had to ride all night to get back to Philadelphia just in time to be the deciding vote in Delaware's 3-man delegation; his co-delegate George Read voted against the Declaration, but ultimately signed the document anyway in a show of support. The New York delegation continued as always to dither on the decision, and abstained (to avoid a negative vote) until it finally voted "yes" later in July after the Declaration had already been formally adopted. Pennsylvania's split delegation voted against the Declaration in an informal July 1st vote; nay-voters John Dickinson and Robert Morris subsequently chose to deliberately miss the official July 2nd vote, a compromise thusly allowing Pennsylvania to vote with the majority for independence while cleverly maintaining the two men's public and historical record of opposition. (Morris was opposed not to independence but to the timing; he subsequently signed the Declaration and became a firm financial supporter of the war.)

On August 2nd, the formal signing ceremony was held, led off with John Hancock's unmistakable signature as President of the Congress. The 55 others followed in order from the northern-most colony (New Hampshire) to the southern-most (Georgia). Some signers actually appended their signatures in the several months after August 2nd due to scheduling or other personal commitments. (Thomas McKean of Delaware did not get around to signing until 1781!) A few delegates refused to sign the document at all given their personal objections. Even the staging of our founding could not follow the intended script perfectly without controversy.

In formulating a revolution, America was destined to establish a new milestone in the development of civilization. Revolutions against rulers over the millennia had typically been reactive, spontaneous explosions acted out by ragtag players forming ad hoc bands of fighters. Not so in America. This instead would be a revolution led by the educated class of the general population (versus the lords and noblemen fighting over ruling succession), framed within philosophy and logic, rationalized by law. It was a very formal and organized revolution, not an outburst by "the rabble" (though the King would see these revolutionaries entirely differently). This would not be another "civil war" of Englishmen against the Crown. Rather, *a separate nation* would be presumed by the revolutionaries, led by a legislative assembly that would document a rational explanation for why their revolution was required and justified. It was all very dressed up and politically correct; nevertheless, just as dangerous and unlikely to succeed as most of the revolutions in history that preceded it. There was nothing before like this kind of revolution in the human experience.

Independence would ultimately come, however, not from legal forms but from the revolutionary fight itself – our noble act was undeniably an act of treason from the vantage point of the King and English law. So this act was more than just a symbolic one; it was genuinely one of great personal risk to each signer. John Hancock and Samuel Adams already had a personal bounty placed on their heads by the English military governor of Boston. So it was left to Franklin, the elder statesman of the Congress, to sum it all up: "[with this Declaration], gentlemen, we must all hang together, or assuredly we shall all hang separately."[9] As it turned out, no signer of the Declaration was hung, nor killed in military service. But some signers did experience personal loss, a few were captured and imprisoned by the English, and most all served the Revolutionary Cause in various ways. A number of signers were subject to personal and/or property attack back home from pro-English Loyalists due to their decision. John Morton (PA), the first signer to die only nine months later, was one such victim of abuse and ostracism from his constituents. Nevertheless, his deathbed message to those who were angered at his voting for independence was: "Tell them that they will live to see the hour when they acknowledge [my vote for independence] to have been the most glorious service I ever rendered to my country."[10] None of the signers ever backed down from the momentous decision that they had made.

Washington fought the war; the 2nd Continental Congress stayed in session to provide a framework and mechanism to support that war. Most of the 56 signers moved on to other endeavors that capitalized on their talents and contributions. Franklin went to France to lobby the French into supporting our struggle. John Adams subsequently joined him, but his always abrasive personality and disdain for French royalty and gaudiness got the best of him and he almost undid Franklin's efforts; he was reassigned to the Netherlands where he successfully negotiated a substantial loan to the Congress. Jefferson went home to Virginia and took a turn as its governor, suffering ridicule when he was forced to flee the capital when the British marched through that state. Some signers returned to their respective colony and assisted with establishing new state and local governments, or served some time in the Continental Army or colonial militia. New delegates to the Congress were appointed as the original signers left.

Many of the signers stayed in the Congress to help with the logistics of the war and the new union of colonies. The 2nd Continental Congress remained in place for the full course of the war, dealing with the everyday mundane issues of needs shared among the 13 colonies – now referred to as "states." They raised funds for the army, procured supplies and weaponry, made military appointments, established inter-state mail services, and guided foreign relations and prospective treaties with other European countries. They did all of this without ever having a written charge defining their Purpose; they did it without a written Constitution delineating their powers and methods. There was no true "national" government, no national court system, no national executive embodying the country. (The "President" of the Congress was elected by that body only to serve a parliamentary position to manage the business of the Congress itself.)

This 2nd Continental Congress had absolutely no power to enforce its decisions, only its limited power of persuasion. Delegates understood that this Congress was a coordinating body on the collective behalf of each of the 13 new states, serving as a "holding function" until the war could be won. Each individual state remained supreme and ran its own internal business without interference. The national needs would all be sorted out later. It was a highly ineffective form of interstate/superstate governance, but given America's history to that point, and the immediate need to fight a war as best as possible, it was the best possible solution that could quickly be put into place.

WINNING THE WAR

"In the language of the Holy Writ, there is a time for all things.
There is a time to preach and a time to fight.
And now is the time to fight."[11]

(John Peter Gabriel Mublenberg,
preacher, in a sermon in 1775 before
leaving to join Washington's troops)

No matter how strong, well-written and effective are the words, words require action. And for the American colonists, action from these words meant prosecuting the war that it had now formally declared. The reasons for the war had been stated, but now the commitment was required. They had promised, "And for the support of this Declaration, with a firm reliance on the protection of Divine Providence, we mutually pledge to each other our lives, our Fortunes, and our sacred Honor." The commitment of the 56 signers of the Declaration was strong; it was a commitment shared by many others; yet commitment was still never universal nor continuous.

The funding of the war was assessed to each colony, but payment was voluntary; some colonies paid and others did not. Washington's army was always struggling for adequate food and arms as a result of this undependable flow of resources. Washington quietly paid for many of his army's needs from his own fortune, and never took a salary for his service. Army recruits and militiamen came and went as domestic needs back home merited their attention, or their resolve melted away in the face of hardships. Holding the army together was a constant concern, best exemplified by the legendary stories of winter encampment at Valley Forge over the brutal winter of 1777-78.

Victory was never assured. Near the end of the War, Washington himself said in a letter to Major General Nathanael Green that, "Posterity would regard as fiction the circumstances under which Americans achieved victory in the War for Independence."[12] By logic, our founding ancestors should never have won this Revolution. In fact, success looked quite fleeting as defeat after defeat piled up, with just enough occasional victories to sustain the spirits of the revolutionaries. Washington freed the Boston blockade, but lost New York City. He defeated a band of Hessian mercenaries in Delaware, but the colonial capital Philadelphia was lost and occupied by the British. Battles in the south went back and forth between victories and defeats until final victory was achieved at Yorktown, Virginia on October 19, 1781 – more than six years after that loud shot heard on Lexington Common. Even the Treaty of Paris formally ending the war took another two years of negotiating among all the parties involved.

V. THE CONFEDERATION CONGRESS

The weaknesses of the 2nd Continental Congress, its lack of a constitutional framework, and its inability to force the colonies to pay for the war effort, were evident almost immediately after the initial euphoria of passing the Declaration of Independence. The focus on prosecuting the war highlighted these shortcomings, but also served to distract potential solutions from being enacted. Nevertheless, the Congress delegates felt the need to put some more defined rules into place, and on July 12, just a week after declaring independence, it authorized a committee to propose a legal framework for its existence. John Dickinson, who had refused to sign the Declaration, nevertheless chaired the drafting committee. That committee came forward with a proposal for a strong central government with very explicit powers in certain key vital areas. For a people just engaged in throwing off the central government of England, such an idea would never be acceptable in that moment. A revised, more limited framework was agreed to by the Congress over a year later on November 15, 1777, then forwarded to the states for adoption. 48 men signed the Articles of Confederation, only 16 of which were also among the 56 who had signed the Declaration of Independence. Already a new wave of the 2nd Founding Fathers had emerged to immediately take responsibility to guide the country to its next phase.

However, even the more limited version of the proposed Articles was not well received by the states. Bickering over the control of valuable western lands, interstate trade and tariffs, the basis of representation to the Congress (small states versus large states), and how the funding of the Congress would be allocated to each state all served to delay ratification. It took almost four years for the states to negotiate their way through these differences. But on

31

March 1, 1781, a final version of the Articles of Confederation was adopted – 7 months before the war ended, and after six years that the 2nd Continental Congress had been in business!

As might be expected at that point in our evolution toward a government, and with the Revolutionary War still in process, these Articles went out of their way to minimize any powers or role for this new "central government" in favor of leaving the power of the states supreme and intact wherever possible. *The provisions of the Confederation articles, and its structure of the Congress, would drive most of the proposals, counter-proposals and discussions for change in the forthcoming Constitutional Convention.* Some of these significant provisions of the Articles provided that:

- This new, united country would be called the "United States of America," the first time this appellation was formally designated.

- The national government for the United States of America would consist solely of a single legislative body. No national executive or court system was provided for. (Congress would elect a "President" only to preside over its activities.)

- Each state would appoint its delegates to the Congress in the manner, number, and based upon the qualifications, that they saw fit.

- Each state would have one collective vote, regardless of population or wealth.

- Most all decisions required 9 of the 13 states to agree (which resulted in little of consequence getting done).

- Amendments to these Articles could only be done by a unanimous vote of the Congress, and then unanimous

<u>ratification</u> by all 13 states. (Resulting in no amendments ever being approved.)

- Congress would have only a <u>limited role and the powers explicitly assigned</u> to it.

- This union of the states under this Confederation agreement would be <u>perpetual</u>.

Congress could not regulate interstate trade or levy taxes on the states or its citizens – leading to interstate trade and tariff wars among the states, and an inability to fund the government's operations or pay off its Revolutionary War debts. The Congress never proved able to speak as *one voice* to other nations. States generally ignored the Congress and did what they wanted; Congress had no enforcement power and no truly *national* standing.

Almost as soon as the Revolutionary War ended, and with it the end of the unifying and driving force that had served to bind the states together in crisis, the weaknesses of this Confederation form of government became more glaringly evident. The individual states were the supreme form of American government, each state politically equal to the other in spite of their inequalities of fact. Giving up that primacy and equality of each state would be a difficult battle to achieve; 200 years later the call for "states' rights" is still a rallying cry for many Americans in spite of having tried such a model in our beginnings.

Yet the Confederation was a good first try at defining a new model for a central government. It was more than a simple "coordinating body" as the Revolutionary Congress had served, but it was well short of being a true national government" empowered to act for the collective good of the people. Even in this form it was a governance model previously unknown in the western world. Its insistence on minimizing any real form of true central authority in favor of state and local government could not be a surprise, given that the country was just emerging from a long and difficult fight to throw off dictatorial centralized rule and to achieve its independence. The rejection of any concept of monarchical authority was alone a unique step to this point in world history. The Articles certainly established some worthwhile precedents for later use, not least of which was the need for written governance at the national level. *But in the end, this particular form of government did not work. It was but a cooperative venture built upon the power of persuasion, not a true union of people and states into some greater whole.* George Washington, himself a victim of Congress's ineffectiveness throughout the war, observed that this Confederation was "little more than a shadow without substance."[1]   And so it was time to acknowledge these shortcomings, and make a new try at this attempt at self-governing.

VI. THE CONSTITUTIONAL CONVENTION

On February 21, 1787, the Confederation Congress approved a call to convene in the following May a convention of delegates from the states. Such a convention would be charged "for the sole and express purpose of revising the Articles of Confederation, and reporting to Congress and the several legislatures such alterations and provisions therein as shall when agreed to in Congress and confirmed by the States, render the federal Constitution adequate to the exigencies of Government and the preservation of the Union."

It was a very specific and limited charge: come up with changes to the Articles that would make that system of government more effective as a national government. But the calling of such a convention was a significant recognition and public acknowledgement of the secret everyone already knew: that the current structure of government under these Articles, with no real power over thirteen independent states, no enforcement ability to raise the funds needed to run the government, no power to enforce agreements among states or establish laws truly common across the nation, and no ability to present America as a common whole internationally, was virtually a farcical exercise. Even if such a convention came up with a set of proposed amendments to these Articles, none could be accepted except by unanimous vote – each state having de facto veto power over virtually any significant proposal before the Congress. But the calls for change had been growing almost since the Articles had been formally adopted six years earlier. And the chorus demanding change was growing louder and more formal. Even if such a convention and the changes they might recommend might threaten the position of the

Congress itself, the calls for change could no longer go unheeded. May 14, 1787 was set as the date for those delegates selected by each state legislature to meet in Philadelphia and see what they could come up with. Seven months later, this Congress, along with the rest of America, would be quite surprised by the announcement from Philadelphia of the design of a whole new form of government. Not just simple changes to what existed, but a virtual 2nd American revolution in its own right – albeit this time a peaceful political one.

This moment in the year 1787, and this Constitutional event, was a critical plateau in the advancement of world civilization, not just America. Americans today face many problems, with solutions to those problems seemingly very elusive. The framework within which we work towards solutions that involve the role of our government comes from the decisions and intentions of these constitutional framers of so long ago – decisions and intentions so often described incorrectly and self-servingly by news commentators and politicians today. If one is going to point to "the Founders" as justification in today's debates, *then it is critical that Americans understand well how this framework came about, the widely diverse thinking of the 55 men who created it, what it truly says (and does not say), and the very practical-minded basis (versus ideological) on which these difficult decisions were based.* Hence in this narrative we must spend extended time focusing on the amazing work done that hot summer in Philadelphia 225 years ago.

THE GATHERING OF DELEGATES

55 men gathered in Philadelphia in response to Congress's Charge and their appointment by their states to represent them in these discussions of revised governance. Like the impressive men that had gathered in the same hall in Philadelphia eleven years earlier that resulted in the writing of the Declaration of Independence, this was an equally impressive lot. But this was a far different cast of players than had assembled in 1776. This was the 3rd wave of American patriots now presenting themselves to the American stage. Only six of them had been signers of the Declaration. (Two of these six had also signed the Articles of Confederation, and two more of these six would ultimately choose *not* to sign the Constitution). Benjamin Franklin (a previous signer) and George Washington (the general) were there, but the rest of the big names of the Revolution that we remember were off performing services to their new country as foreign ambassadors (e.g. Thomas Jefferson and John Adams), or governors or state legislators, or other needed roles for the country (e.g. Patrick Henry, Richard Henry Lee and Francis Lightfoot Lee, Samuel Adams, John Hancock).

But these delegates had all proven their intellectual worthiness and loyalty to the country either as 2nd-tier soldiers in the Revolutionary War, in functional governmental service, or in a variety of political roles during and subsequent to the War's end. 42 of the delegates had served at one time or another in the Continental Congress, giving them an important firsthand understanding of the present difficulties of governance, yet only 18 were currently serving in that body versus performing other political roles. 27 of the 55 were under the age of 50; 14 under the age of 40 (the youngest was 27). They were unequal in number from each state – eight from Pennsylvania, seven from Virginia; as few as three from New York; only two of four appointed delegates from New Hampshire ever showed up; and Rhode Island, fearful of losing control of its destiny and disproportionate power given its being the smallest state, boycotted the convention entirely and sent zero delegates, thus having no impact on the Constitution at all. A number of delegates arrived well after the Convention's business commenced; a few others left early before the Constitution was finalized. Regardless of the number of appointed delegates, each state had only one collective vote (continuing the equal states precedence in the Confederation Congress). These delegates were from various backgrounds of wealth, profession, and service; many were lawyers, others were planters, physicians, and businessmen; 25 owned slaves (not all of these were southerners), and all had either war or political experience in their resumes (see Appendix 1).

In spite of their differences of background, they shared a love of their new country, an appreciation of the opportunities before it, an often first-hand awareness of the shortcomings of the current government under the Articles, and they were committed to bettering it. They were all well educated, with 29 having formal undergraduate degrees, and 29 also having studied law to varying extents. They knew the relevant lessons of the histories of governments, church, kings/royalty, and war from the ancient worlds through the recent histories of England and the European continent. The high effort and terrible toll America had paid to separate itself from England, the King and a distant government "interfering in their business" was always forefront in their minds; those lessons would be well reflected in the writing of their new Constitution. Jefferson referred to these delegates as "an assembly of demi-gods"; Robert Morris (PA) more humbly referred to the outcome as simply the work of "plain, honest men." (Morris's description of "Plain, Honest Men" also served as the title for historian Richard Beeman's excellent in-depth telling of the inside story of the Convention and its delegates principally based upon the private notes of the Convention maintained by James Madison.)

What the delegates did not share coming into Philadelphia was a pre-disposed, shared vision for a particular solution. A few (led by Virginia with Pennsylvania quickly coming on board) came armed with a plan ready to be presented for immediate consideration by the Convention. Others came open to listening to ideas and willing to be led to a reasoned conclusion. Still others came prepared to ensure that change would be limited and non-threatening to the existing political and/or economic interests of their states. If a stronger national government was assumed to be needed, *how strong* would be the central question to be answered. If the commitment to their charge was high, the depth of their differences on the specific changes to be made was deep, and would show up almost immediately.

For various reasons (travel delays, bad weather, late appointments made, lack of interest by some delegates or their states, etc.), the Convention did not open as scheduled on May 14 due to a lack of a quorum. It was an inauspicious start to what would be such an auspicious outcome, but perhaps predicted the difficulty that would be encountered in completing this important work. Yet for the Virginia delegates (led by James Madison) and Pennsylvania delegates (led by Gouverneur Morris and James Wilson) already in Philadelphia by this time, the delay allowed them time to meet informally, exchange ideas, find common ground, and strategize prior to the Convention opening. These were the two richest and most populated states in the Union, and their delegates had radical ideas for major changes in the government of the United States. They would get organized, work together and be ready.

THE WORK COMMENCES

Finally, on May 25, 1787, sufficient delegates from seven of the states had made it to town to open the Convention for business. (A number of delegates continued to trickle in through the end of June; the last delegate to attend, Daniel Carroll from Maryland, did not arrive until August 6th and only stayed for eleven days!) The first order of business? As it has been since pre-historic times, elect a leader. And this leader would be, not surprisingly, George Washington – the most admired person of his day throughout the country. Serving as Commanding General of the Continental Army for eight years had kept Washington out of a political / legislative role since taking command of the army; his election as Presiding Officer of the Convention now brought him back into a governmental role. His election was unanimous, as expected. Washington would speak little during the course of the Convention, and he would keep his political views very private during all of the debates. But his commanding presence and leadership stature ensured that the proceedings would have the dignity, credibility and recognition of importance needed for the task at hand.

William Jackson (SC), not a delegate but a former secretary to Washington during the war, was then elected as the Convention's secretary, responsible for keeping the written record of the proceedings and votes. It was an unfortunate choice, as Jackson's recordkeeping skills were abysmal. Based upon his disorganized and incomplete records, we would know next to nothing about the events and discussions of the proceedings. Fortunately for history, James Madison (VA) kept detailed personal notes of each day's events; it is to these notes that historians look to for understanding how the Constitution evolved from this gathering of delegates. This source became even more crucial when early on the delegates pledged to keep their deliberation strictly secret so that their discussions could be conducted without undue pressure and interference from outsiders. It was a good decision considering the extreme and varied options that they considered and ultimately adopted versus their original charge. *Secrecy served as a protective shield to encourage the delegates to risk controversial ideas, change opinions (and votes), and explore the ideas of their contemporaries. It is highly doubtful that they would ever have wound up with such an original and creative output had their every word been subject to public examination along the way.* Thomas Jefferson, then serving as ambassador to France, decried that such governmental planning was happening in secrecy, out of the public view. However, his protégé James Madison later reflected that "no Constitution would ever have been adopted by the Convention if the debates had been public."[1] Even George Washington as Convention President, when he found a copy of someone's notes left carelessly on the floor, stated to the assembly that "I must entreat the gentlemen to be more careful, lest our transactions get into the news papers, and disturb the public repose by premature speculations."[2]

What is remarkable in this current day of self-serving "anonymous leaks" and "as reported by an official close to the situation who requested anonymity as he was not authorized to speak on this issue" (but who chose to speak nonetheless!) was that these delegates were men of their word – there was no recorded leak made known during the entire four months of the session. (Some delegates did opt to publish their recollections after the Convention concluded.) Given that secrecy, and as we acknowledge that some of his notes may be understandingly self-selected or somewhat biased, Madison's private record nevertheless offers us the only real log of who said what, when, and to what outcome.

The only remaining business of the first day was to certify each delegate's authority to represent their state and to listen to some opening speeches from some of the delegates. All of the state mandates concurred with the need for changes to the current form

41

of national government, and all assumed a greater authority for that government. However, a short speech by George Read (DE) quietly set the marker for the conflicts to come when he stated that his state of Delaware had specifically restricted its delegates from altering the Confederation's provision that each state had the same number of votes in the Congress – i.e. that all states, regardless of size or wealth, would be equal in the national decision-making. Protecting the integrity and power of each state's own self-interest, a shortcoming that was already dooming the Confederation, wasted no time on Day 1 in rearing its ugly head at this convention that was intended to strengthen that union. Given that the delegates agreed that each state would have an equal vote in the Convention's decisions, the early announcement that small-state Delaware would fight any loss of its national influence was seen as a serious consideration to the upcoming deliberations.

The delegates appointed some standing committees to organize the business and the working rules of the group and then adjourned. After all the delays encountered thus far, just getting underway was enough for this first day.

VII. THE DIVIDING ISSUES

With the organizing business taken care of, it was time for the Convention to begin consideration of the substance. What specific changes should be proposed to the Articles of Confederation? How should a revised national government look compared to the current model? It would be the Virginia delegation that would get the conversation started, and with a very big bang.

Edmund Randolph, governor of the richest and most populous state of Virginia, presented "the Virginia Plan" to the delegates. It was the first of several plans that would ultimately be presented in order to try to find agreement among the various views and factions. This plan was largely the work of James Madison prior to the opening of the Convention. Madison was an early and continued advocate of calling this Convention together. His advance work in already having a model developed, his dedicated note-taking and organizing influence on the deliberations, and his willingness to seek compromise in order to achieve the ultimate end – a new constitution for a strengthened central government – all led to his subsequent sobriquet as "The Father of the Constitution," even though the final version of his Constitution was dramatically different than this original plan first submitted.

The Virginia Plan contained several key elements:

- A powerful legislature would consist of two houses (similar to the design of the British Parliament, but a change from the single body used in the Continental and Confederation Congresses).

- Representation in both houses would be apportioned based upon the relative population of "free inhabitants" of each

43

state (thus ending the "equality of states" idea, the hallmark of the Confederation).

- The lower house would be elected directly by the voting population rather than by the state legislatures (the definition of "free inhabitants" and the eligibility to vote being determined by each state).

- The upper house would be elected by the lower house and provide a check on the lower house elected by the masses (as well as ensure that both legislative bodies would be free of allegiance to the state legislatures).

- The [untitled] executive – which could be an individual or a committee – would simply serve as the administrator for Congress' laws and instructions, and therefore would be selected and directed by Congress (rather than the people), thereby simply being an extension of the all-powerful Congress.

- A judiciary would be established to determine legal questions, with some power of veto over the legislature, but not much detail about this group was delineated.

- Congress would have the power to veto any state law deemed not in the interest of the combined union.

- A Council of Revision would be established consisting of the executive(s) and selected members of the judiciary who could review any law passed by Congress or the states with the right of veto.

This proposal struck at the heart of the sovereignty of the states, significantly reduced the current role of the state legislatures in managing the national congress, eliminated the equal status of the states among themselves, and made the states decidedly inferior to the national congress. It was a complete upending of the primacy and equality of the states that had existed up to this time. And it openly proposed a strong central government fresh on the heels of

44

a Revolution against centralized rule that had formally ended only four years previously. It was an audacious first offering, to say the least. It was far beyond the original charge to simply come up with proposed amendments to the Articles and far beyond the expectations of most of the delegates then present. And in the end it would not fly. But it would serve to crystallize the issues, surface the differing perspectives, and jumpstart the discussions quite effectively. And it would lead to an early decision by the Convention to adopt a resolution that "a national government ought to be established consisting of a supreme legislative, executive and judiciary." That decision committed the delegates to scrap the Articles of Confederation entirely, and to come up with an entirely new form of government for the Union.

Over the course of the next four months, the principal thorny issues that would emerge to divide the delegates and dominate their deliberations were:

- Trust in the common person – whether to be a democracy or representative government, and how far to extend "enfranchisement"

- Succession and term lengths – ending the "divine right" of rulers

- Representation in the legislative body – how to balance "majority rules" versus "minority rights"

- Role of the executive officer – leadership without monarchy

- Distribution of powers – how to allocate roles and authority among all of the independent yet interdependent governmental units: the national government, the different branches of the national government, and the states

- Slavery – reconciling economic dependency with human rights

ISSUE 1: TRUST OF THE COMMON PERSON

Underlying most all discussions and decisions of the Convention delegates was what should be the role and relationship of the common person in this new government. The delegates were committed to protecting and ensuring the freedom of the common citizen (although as it turned out, not all of the people would be ensured *equal* freedoms). And they understood that men had fought in the Revolutionary War in order to be free of governmental domination. But thousands of years of royal/aristocratic rule do not fade easily from perceptions of the proper structuring of government. So was this to be a *democratic* government, wherein people govern themselves directly? Or a representative (*republican*) form of government, where a selected few govern on behalf of the many?

In spite of our wistful yet false view looking back from the 21st century, the reality was that *most all of the delegates found the idea of the common person directly participating in the government to be a frightening, if not incomprehensible concept.* The sheer expanse of the size of the country – already bigger than most all of the European states – was seen to preclude an understanding by the common person of national (versus local parochial) issues of the day or the ability to discern the truly qualified men for government. Besides, the working people would not have time or interest in being informed as to these things. Nor did they have sufficient education to understand the finer points of issues or laws. Roger Sherman (CT), a normally well-reasoned thinker, stated on the idea of the direct election of the president by the people, "The people at large will never be sufficiently informed to make a wise choice." Or more generally, that "the people … should have as little to do as may be about the government. They want information and are constantly liable to be misled."[1] George

Mason (VA), in more acerbic tones, stated bluntly that the direct popular election of a president "would be the equivalent of referring a trial of colors to a blind man."[2]

There were, however, some proponents for the competency of the common people. James Wilson (PA) was a primary advocate for democratic approaches on most all issues. His colleague Benjamin Franklin (PA), much venerated for his genuine sentiment and seasoned perspective though most often ignored in his substantive proposals, held much more faith in the common man, a faith based upon Pennsylvania governance from its earliest founding. Out of respect for this common person, Franklin admonished at one point that "It is of great consequence that we should not depress the virtue and public spirit of our common people, of which they displayed a great deal during the war, and which contributed principally to the favorable issue of it."[3] And when talk would so frequently tend to favor the elite citizenry as being the only people qualified to be leaders of the country, Franklin observed that "Some of the greatest rogues I was ever acquainted with were the richest rogues."[4]

Nevertheless, on most issues regarding government structuring, distribution of power, how individuals should be elected, who should have voting power, or who should even be eligible for holding government office, the common person was often shunted out of that spotlight. Originally, there was much sentiment and discussion around restricting voting (i.e. citizenship), and/or the eligibility to hold office, to land-owners only. Gouverneur Morris (PA), a decidedly very rich man, said that "Give the votes to people who have no property, and they will sell them to the rich who will be able to buy them."[5] He went on to further state that "The ignorant and the dependent can be as little trusted with the public interest as small children."[6] But too many other versions of wealth existed, so this narrow treatment of property ownership was deemed unworkable. Ultimately, voter qualifications were simply left to the states to decide for their constituent population.

In fairness to them, it was understood by the delegates that this new government emanated from, and was for the benefit of, "We the People ..." But in the end, the patronizing view of the majority of those delegates was that those people needed some measure of protection from themselves. Requirements of age and residency were seen as fair restrictions. *But real democracy (i.e. direct elections and eligibility for office), extended to all of the people regardless of wealth, property ownership, education, race or gender, would have to wait another couple of hundred of years (and apparently beyond) before true equality would be genuinely realized.*

ISSUE 2: DIVINE RIGHT AND SUCCESSION

In all their deliberations, the delegates were committed, either intuitively or through the course of their discussions, to ending two of the real failures of royal government over the centuries: 1) the "divine right of kings," and 2) succession by right of birth. While these delegates were religious individuals in their communities, all affiliated with some branch of the Christian faith, with a few expressing a sense of divine engagement guiding this Convention and its proceedings, they nevertheless adamantly viewed their work as a secular creation for the benefit of the people. Government was a secular enterprise of and for the people. The presumption of a king's right to rule being a divine calling or godly permission was the antithesis of a "people's government." These delegates were committed to putting an end to any such presumptions by insisting that all holding of offices would come by "appointment" (election) from the people – even if (as described above) such appointments would come through some intermediary forum. Further, there would be no automatic succession to the holder of an office on the basis of birthright.

48

Other than if necessary for a temporary transition period (e.g. the Vice President assuming the office in the event of the president's death), all succession of office would be by fresh election or appointment. Succession by birthright had long been proven to allow unqualified persons, or persons undesirable to the citizenry, into positions of great responsibility with disastrous results and no remedy other than war. For this new form of government, every effort and method would be employed to ensure that only qualified persons would manage governmental affairs – even if such concerns would for a time overly exclude desirable persons of worth.

As a result of their solutions to their concerns, America has enjoyed 225 years of peaceful transitions of power across its national government, even in instances where the results may have been hotly contested and decided by the thinnest of voting margins. There have in fact been only three instances of "family succession" for the office of President, and in all instances there were intervening holders of that office: John Adams and his son John Quincy Adams; William Henry Harrison and his grandson Benjamin Harrison; George Herbert Walker Bush and his son George Walker Bush. (Theodore and Franklin Roosevelt were cousins). America has always had many versions of family political dynasties, each making greater or lesser contributions to America, but none have managed to take unelected control over the government.

As another aspect to the issue of succession, delegates also applied rules of fixed terms on office occupants (excluding judges) rather than kings ruling for their lifetime. There were many different proposals for what these proper limits should be as regarded each particular office, whether reelection should be allowed, and what powers the office should have vis-à-vis the length of term of that office. It was also important to balance the need for stability in government (longer terms) with the need to ensure that office holders would be held quickly accountable at the ballot box

49

(shorter terms). The solution to innumerable proposals for terms and limits came when the delegates began to look not at the structuring of each individual office, but when they looked at the emerging government as a complete design. That allowed them to put into place a comprehensive structure *across* the whole scheme that would balance their fears of governmental or individual officeholder domination. Hence they would balance a House term of two years (responsive accountability), with a Senate term of six years (stability), with a Presidential term of four years (compromise between accountability and stability), and a lifetime appointment for judges (independence from any political hysteria of the moment).   All would be eligible for reelection, and impeachment would serve as a protective force against malfeasance.

ISSUE 3: REPRESENTATION

As we saw, the first highly divisive issue to immediately emerge was how representation in the government would be allocated. The big states of Virginia and Pennsylvania, looking out for their own interests, favored that population (and/or wealth) should be the basis for representation in the new Congress, ending the past precedent of equal status for each state.   Delaware, Connecticut and New Jersey recoiled against this idea, intent on preserving the equal status of each state regardless of size, expecting that the other smaller populated states such as Maryland, New Hampshire and Georgia would be of like mind once they arrived at the Convention (plus Rhode Island if it ever chose to participate).

Debate on this first issue went on for months and hung over all discussion of any other parts of a constitutional plan.   Various versions of an approach came and went without agreement.   On this one issue it appeared that the Convention would likely fail.

Finally a working committee introduced a revised version of a "Connecticut Plan" that had been previously offered in early June by Roger Sherman (CT), revised with some modifications that had been suggested by Benjamin Franklin, leaving some details and clarifications to be worked out later. It was a "split the difference with a carrot" approach to compromise that included:

- Representation in the lower body (House of Representatives) would be by population. This body was said to represent "the people," and supported "the majority rules" proposition. (It is to fulfill this apportionment-by-population requirement that we undergo a mandatory census of our population every ten years.)

- Representation in the upper body (Senate) would be "equal." Whether there would be one vote per state, multiple senators per state but only one collective state vote, or having an equal number of senators for each state but each able to vote independently was left for later discussion. This body was said to represent "the states," and protected "the minority rights" proposition.

- As an incentive to the large states to support this 2-part approach, the lower house that was based on population would have the sole right to originate bills involving raising or spending governmental money, thereby protecting the wealthier states from undue demands of financial support that might be pushed by the smaller states.

Nevertheless, positions for proportional representation versus equal representations did not die easily, and positions hardened in several of the leading delegates. The small states were generally comfortable with the proposed compromise; it gave them some reasonable defense against being overwhelmed in the Congress. The proportional adherents adamantly continued to insist unbendingly on proportional representation in both houses. It therefore took until July 23 for the question to be finally settled.

For most of the delegates, the rejection of an either/or debating position and the acceptance of this compromise was driven by an understanding that the whole Convention could easily blow up over a failure to resolve this one fundamental question. But *they were more committed to the larger goal of solving a pressing governance problem* (the Confederation's shortcomings) *than they were to interminably arguing over absolute principle and failing on the larger point.* (Unfortunately, this commitment to compromise so as to achieve results is missing from our present national conversation.) So to the relief of most, they made a practical decision of a reasonable compromise for both positions. But it would remain a contentious issue, continually resurfacing even though thought settled, until near the very end of the Convention.

ISSUE 4: THE NATIONAL EXECUTIVE

The original Virginia Plan envisioned the chief executive officer of the national government to be little more than an administrator selected by, subservient and reporting to, the legislative body. But Madison himself admitted that he had really given little detailed thought to this role, concentrating more on the assumed primacy of the legislative function. Yet other delegates were concerned about continuing with a weak executive office such as existed under the Articles of Confederation. For some, the essence of the issue revolved around a fundamental question: if the legislature represented the interests and perspectives of the individual states, who would represent and speak for the nation as a greater whole?

Fears of the old English monarchy, and the record of the thousands of years of kings before this latest King of England, lay underneath all debates about a "chief magistrate." Those fears ultimately spurred the requirement that this chief executive be a natural-born citizen of the United States to hopefully dilute any old European influence within this individual, and to assure that he would be steeped in "the American tradition." Yet other than a "president" who was little more than a presiding officer over the legislature, there was really no other known example for what a non-royal / non-dictator leader might look like. This would have to be worked out from scratch. Washington, from the advantage of his war-time experience as a respected and trusted leader, proved to be a major force in calling the question about the executive role. But as was his tendency (and proper for his role as the president of the Convention), he offered little detailed suggestions for how the office should be constructed.

Virginia's original plan called for a single person to serve as the National Executive, chosen by the legislature (Congress), to serve for seven years, ineligible for a subsequent term, removable upon malpractice or neglect of duty, charged with carrying out the nation's laws and running the inevitable bureaucracy, and to receive a fixed salary for his services from the national treasury. Settling on one individual to serve in the role (versus a committee) gained acceptance fairly easily from the majority of delegates. How to *select* that individual proved more contentious:

- should the National Executive be selected by an informed Congress on behalf of the more untrustworthy people at large (a republican view), or should that selection be made directly by the people who the Executive was charged with representing (a democratic view)?

- could the citizens of such a vastly sized country, with such differences in local cultures and economic portfolios, be capable of understanding and properly selecting from among the potential candidates for the executive office?

- what approach would best give the executive the correct measure of independence from the legislature, yet keep that individual in check from assuming monarchical, centralized power?

- what powers, authority and term should this individual have?

- should the decision turn on old, historical fears, or on new, future promises?

Once again, the debate on this subject was protracted, with debate extending almost to the very end of the Convention. Near the conclusion of the Convention, James Wilson (PA) observed that "This subject [of how to elect the president] has greatly divided the Convention and will also divide people out of doors. It is in truth the most difficult of all on which we have to decide."[7] Given that less advance thought had been given to this design topic, and they were working from more of a blank slate with no real models to emulate (other than *not* installing a king!), numerous proposals were offered for how the National Executive office should ultimately be structured.

The primary issue regarding the executive office was how to select that individual (having rejected fairly easily the idea of a committee as the executive). The fight over an election method centered around who could be trusted with the wisdom, insight and judgment to do the electing. Some delegates supported the idea of election directly by the voters (the truly democratic approach). But many more delegates simply did not trust the capability of the vast electorate to make such an important decision, or feared that the citizenry could be "easily duped" into making a poor choice, or would simply focus on local concerns rather than overriding Union concerns (even though the "educated class" had frequently proved themselves no more capable of "big picture" thinking than the common man!). Rather, most of these delegates felt that only an educated and informed group of leaders could be relied on to make a good choice (the representative approach). But regardless of what group would be charged with making the selection, how do you then ensure that the executive would be sufficiently independent and not overly beholden to that group?

To solve the vexing election method question, a proposal was offered that *a separate group of electors would be elected by the people; this group of electors would then vote to select the Executive and immediately disband, having no permanent function.* This approach gave the starting point to the people, but still entrusted the final decision to a group assumed to be more capable of making a good selection. A later version of this approach kept the idea of the separate body of electors, but gave their election to the state legislatures. A different approach proposed that the governors of the states appoint the electors. Innumerable other ideas were floated to the Convention at one time or another, often multiple times as the delegates struggled to find an answer. However, all of the suggested approaches took Congress out of the selection process. None of these approaches gained immediate favor, and for a time the original proposal of election by the Congress remained the default approach. But the idea of electing a distinctly separate body to in turn vote for the National Executive remained quietly in background for a while, destined to show up again in the final deliberations.

For the term of service for this National Executive, the Virginia Plan had called for a single term of seven years. But the specter of such a National Executive morphing into an "American King" would underlie discussions about this new office for some time. At one point Hugh Williamson (NC) reflected that "it was pretty certain ... that we should at some time or other have a King, but he wished no precaution be omitted that might postpone the event as long as possible."[8] Williamson's solution to his own problem was to support proposals to limit the executive to one term of seven years. Another proposal was made for a single term of six years; proposals of 11 years and 15 years tenure were also offered up. James McClurg (VA) proposed instead to make the term one of "during good behavior," effectively making it a lifetime appointment – a very kingly proposition. As expected, this near-monarchical suggestion went down to defeat rather quickly. Ultimately, unlimited terms of four years each would be adopted.

But such a "radical" suggestion as McClurg's fortunately caused many delegates to think more seriously about what exactly this office should be about. The more power it had the more there was a need for care in who that person would be and how that person should be selected. If the role was as originally envisioned – simply a lackey to an all-powerful Congress – then such concerns would be less important. But for a growing number of delegates, the thinking grew to make the National Executive more independent of Congress, therefore the need to find another method for this selection than by Congress. Even McClurg's Virginia colleague Madison, originally the author of the Congressional-based approach, came to admit that a union of executive and legislative functions was a bad idea, with the conclusion that the two should be kept distinct and independent of one another.

The need for a defined and orderly method (other than by war or revolution) to remove the National Executive for an abuse of power gradually came to also be seen as a necessity, even though the office would be of a fixed term allowing for continuation only upon reelection. The problem was agreeing on wording for what offenses should be appropriate for impeachment without making the office subject to trivial acts and political whim, and what mechanism(s) for removal should be employed. The whole idea of executive impeachment itself was once again chartering a path into new territory. There was no historical precedence for the removal of a national executive by trial or process versus resorting to armed revolt, and Americans had already gone the armed revolt route to remove themselves from King George. That experience confirmed to them that, human beings being what they are, the improper use of high political offices would always be a potential. But a less costly and disruptive method of addressing that malfeasance by utilizing an impeachment method was required. In the end, there have only been two instances of presidential impeachment proceedings, neither of which resulted in conviction: Andrew Johnson, the successor to the assassinated Abraham Lincoln, in 1868 during the Civil War Reconstruction period (it failed by one vote); and Bill Clinton in 1998-1999 over charges of perjury and obstruction of justice that many felt were politically motivated (it failed substantially, with voting along party lines).

It was over half-way through the Convention before the "National Executive" became called the "President," probably the easiest decision made regarding this office. Defining the American Presidency would remain a challenge to the delegates all through the Convention. The negatives driving its formation would come from their experience and their fears; the positives would come from their reasoning and their hopes. In the end, they would give defining the form their best shot, and the substance of the office would come from actual practice by its first occupant – George Washington.

ISSUE 5: DISTRIBUTION OF POWERS

Under the Articles of Confederation, the states were clearly the primary basis of governmental power. The Congress of a single body (with no separate executive or judiciary) was merely a place where the independent and sovereign states could meet and identify any common concerns, and determine if they wished to act jointly on such concerns. In that sense, the Confederation government was much akin to our present-day United Nations, or perhaps even the European Union – two essentially toothless tigers able to act only with the permission of their constituent sovereign member states. The Confederation was often described as a "federal" system – governance shared between the collective Congress and the individual 13 states – but it was really no governance at all. It was certainly not a "national" government –

one unit exercising governance over all the people, with the states serving a merely functional role as subordinate districts for implementing such national policies.

For a few delegates, a toothless Congress was a perfectly desirable arrangement that should be kept. For most, however, a more evenly balanced structure was needed. At one point Alexander Hamilton (NY) proposed a sweeping plan of centralized power that effectively eliminated state power and created instead a truly national government. The Congress would look very similar to the English Parliament; the National Executive would serve for life and have absolute veto power over legislation; state governors would be appointed by Congress, who would also have veto power over state legislatures. This proposal swung too far in the extreme of a national structure, and was too reminiscent of the English government Americans had just rejected. It essentially consigned Hamilton's ideas to being ignored for the remainder of the Convention – and to a lifetime of distrust from the more conservative pro-state factions. "Federal supremacy" had been agreed to early on, but few had any idea of what it substantively meant. Clarity, and fairly specific clarity at that, would be needed to assuage the collective concerns.

National Government Versus State Governments
Once the question of proportional representation in the Congress was resolved in a compromise favorable to the small states, most of these delegates then opted to support the establishment of a strong central government. Nevertheless, one early recognition was that a Congressional veto over state laws would never fly with the state governments, would be impractical and cumbersome to implement, and would likely derail the adoption of any new constitution. The middle ground adopted was that *Congressional laws would be supreme over the laws of the individual states, but states would be left free to go their own way as long as they did not conflict with Congress' laws*. (The federal judiciary would

ultimately prove to be the key player in overseeing this compromise.)

Further, the delegates realized that overly-broad wordings as to what legislative concerns would be within Congress' sphere versus the states would need far more specificity in order to sell this Constitution to the suspicious states and a wary populace. So they included a specific listing of Congress' authorized powers plus some powers specifically prohibited to the states in the final document – not without considerable line-by-line debate, of course. Yet as time would ultimately show, given the sensitivity and criticality of this question, even such a specific delineation of Congress' powers would still leave much room for multiple conflicting interpretations, particularly with respect to two clauses:

- "The Congress shall have Power to lay and collect Taxes … to pay the Debts and *provide for the common Defence and general Welfare of the United States …*" (*italics added*);

- "To make all *Laws which shall be necessary and proper* for carrying into Execution the foregoing Powers, and all other Powers vested by this Constitution in the Government of the United States, or in any Department or Officer thereof" (*italics added*).

The broad wording of these two clauses in effect counterbalanced all the more narrowly specified clauses which were otherwise listed. They subsequently opened the door for a broad expansion of Congressional jurisdiction for what is required to "provide for the general welfare" or what is "necessary and proper" for Congress to meet its governing responsibilities. Notwithstanding the never-ending 200 years of arguments over the "correct" interpretation of these two clauses, in the end room was found for both a state and a national form of government to reasonably coexist – our <u>federal</u> system.

59

Congress Versus President

As concerned as they were about concentrating too much power in a president, the concern about a runaway Congress grew increasingly on the minds of the delegates. While legislative governance was the familiar form, there was also a wide view that experience had shown that legislatures in the individual states were fickle arenas, had often overstepped their authority and abilities in favor of self-interests, and were not wholly reliable. Having a strong president independent of the Congress was seen as an effective way to put a check on Congress, but the question remained of how that individual should be elected so as to still be accountable himself. Many delegates were willing to move away from having Congress elect the president, but despite many proposals offered up for discussion, they could not come around to agree on any alternative approach.

The initial, longstanding trend favoring Congress to elect the president dissolved as the list of presidential powers grew. John Dickinson (DE) warned that "the powers which we have agreed to vest in the President were so many and so great" that people would demand "they themselves be more immediately concerned in [the President's] election."[9] Finally, only weeks before the Convention's end, the decision was made to go back to the Roger Sherman (CT) plan offered in June for a separate body of electors (subsequently referred to as the "Electoral College"), with these electors to be chosen however each state legislature determined (e.g. by popular vote, or by the legislature itself). To break the next logjam of whether the House or the Senate should be the backup in the event that no candidate would achieve a majority vote in the Electoral College, a last-minute breakthrough proposal (also from Roger Sherman) was that the House would make the choice, but it would have <u>one vote per state</u>. This very creative solution combined the "representative of the people" feature of the House with the "equal states" feature of the Senate. The Senate would then be left with the job of choosing the Vice President.

A number of delegates feared that the Electoral College concept would never work and that most all elections would wind up in the House. But by now they were tired of the issue and getting near the end of their deliberations, so this approach sounded good and was adopted. (Many of these details have since been changed by subsequent constitutional amendments.)

As it turned out, the much maligned Electoral College has done its intended job of providing an interim means between a representative election with a protection of states' interests. In our history of 56 presidential elections between 1788 and 2008, there have been only <u>two</u> instances of elections being thrown to the House to decide. In the 1800 election between Thomas Jefferson and Aaron Burr, each tied for electoral votes, requiring 36 votes to be taken in the House in order to declare Jefferson the winner. The 1824 election was fought among John Quincy Adams, Andrew Jackson, and two other candidates. Jackson had won the popular vote and received a plurality of electoral votes, but amid accusations of "deal making" the House selected Adams after only one vote was taken.

There have also been a few close calls in presidential elections. In 1876 Rutherford B. Hayes received a one electoral vote majority amid accusations of disputed elector credentials, versus Samuel Tilden who had won the popular vote. This election provoked accusations of a backroom deal made to effectively end the Reconstruction Period and its punitive laws towards the South after the Civil War. Subsequent actions by Hayes appeared to confirm the accusations. And in 2000 George W. Bush received a five electoral vote majority versus Al Gore who had won the popular vote. That year's highly disputed election results required a first-time intervention by the Supreme Court into deciding the election of a President, this instance based upon a <u>judicial</u> review of irregular voting processes in Florida.

Besides this Congressional backup role in the electing of the president, the Constitution gave a veto power over legislation to the President, but it was not absolute; balancing authority was given to Congress to override such a veto by a two-thirds vote in each house. The President was also required "from time to time to give information to Congress on the state of the Union." This requirement leads to today's annual spectacle in January of the televised State of the Union address to Congress outlining the President's view of the current issues and needs of the country, and the goals and legislation the President wishes to be pursued during the year.

House Versus Senate

The real distinctions between the House and the Senate centered more around who would sit in each respective body versus differences in what they would do. The House, based upon proportional representation and elected in total every two years, was seen as the body more connected to the people and more quickly responsive to demands of the majority for change in direction. The Senate, based upon equal state representation and elected every six years on a $1/3^{rd}$ rotating basis, was seen as the "calmer head" body of more distinguished and wiser legislators who would protect the rights of the minority (smaller) states. It was quick responsiveness in the House balanced with thoughtful deliberation in the Senate.

Other than those distinctions of form, both bodies were assumed to individually fulfill similar legislative roles, coming together at the end of their respective deliberations to work out their different perspectives – *thereby emulating the need for the country to come together and work out its differences of perspectives respecting majority rules versus minority rights.* A few distinctions in function were allocated between the two bodies. The House was given authority to originate financial bills; some Convention delegates had sought to disallow the Senate to change these House bills and vote only "yea or nay," but the final decision was that the Senate could only either concur with or seek to alter those bills. The Senate was given the power to approve international treaties and appointments to the cabinet made by the President. The House initiates any impeachment proceedings for "Treason, Bribery, or other high Crimes and Misdemeanors"; the Senate tries the case with a two-thirds vote required for conviction, and the Chief Justice serves as the trial judge. In essence, there were not a lot of differences between the roles of these two bodies once the highly divisive question of representation was settled.

Judiciary Role

A national judiciary was the least considered, and thereby least defined role in the final Constitution. The need for a multi-tiered judiciary within the national government was assumed, with such being the arbiter of national legal questions and supremacy over any conflicts in state judicial proceedings. But there was not a lot of thought about its scope or structure. The delegates' principal goal was to establish an *independent* judiciary, given their experiences of dependent judiciaries in Europe beholden to the King, all too often merely rubber-stamping his wishes or trampling over the right of due process for the citizenry. But as with all things they did not want the judiciary (or any other arm of government) to be *too* independent. Hence controls would need to be in place: while appointed for life to ensure judicial stability and integrity, judges would also be subject to impeachment; constitutional amendments could be passed to negate the findings of a judicial review. *Ultimately it would be the courts themselves who would define their role through actual practice, built upon the high respect and honor Americans have for the rule of law.*

The delegates did resist giving the judiciary any involvement in the *making* of laws or deciding on the *value* (i.e. were they good or bad policy) of laws. (Madison had in fact promoted just such a qualitative role for the judiciary as a joint responsibility with the

President through a "Council of Revision" to review all laws passed by Congress.) But delegates did assume that the judiciary were the ones to determine the *legality* (i.e. constitutionality) of a law, <u>although that power does not explicitly appear anywhere in the Constitution</u>. Such a power would ultimately be simply self-servingly presumed and affirmed by the Supreme Court itself in 1803. When it made its first declaration of a law as unconstitutional, Chief Justice John Marshall simply declared that the Court in fact had that inferred responsibility as a natural extension of its overall role in the government. Neither Congress nor then-President Thomas Jefferson (as big an opponent of big government as there ever was) protested the Court's decision and rationale. The precedence was thereby forever accepted by their non-action. Such an inference was not unwarranted. Delegate Luther Martin (MD) had stated during the discussions of the judiciary that "As to the constitutionality of laws, that point will come before the judges in their proper official character."[10] And John Rutledge (SC) said that "Judges ought never to give their opinion on a law until it comes before them,"[11] affirming that the judiciary should have no enacting role in the law but did have a presumed after-the-fact determination responsibility.

The manner of selecting judges was essentially an argument over whether it should be a power of the President or Congress; the inevitable compromise was Presidential nomination and Senate approval. The scope of the judiciary's jurisdiction is explicitly defined in the Constitution and quite comprehensive, but as we have noted it is mainly a review / appellate / legality function. The requirement that all trials would be "by jury" was also affirmed, and would subsequently be strengthened within the Bill of Rights that came later. Otherwise, not much else about the judiciary was specified in the Constitution.

ISSUE 6: SLAVERY

For all their contentious, continual debates on virtually every proposal and detail that was presented to the delegates, there were really only two "line in the sand" issues that confronted their deliberations and threatened failure to achieve a new Constitution. One was the representation issue for the legislature, pitting the highly populated states against the smaller states. That was ultimately resolved by having two houses of Congress: the House based upon relative population, the Senate by equal representation for each state.

The second such defining issue revolved around slavery. It emerged as a moral issue, a cultural issue, a regional issue, a property issue, and a population issue. Almost half of the delegates across north and south owned slaves, from as little as a few household slaves (e.g. Robert Morris-PA; James Wilson-PA; William Johnson-CT; William Paterson-NJ) to hundreds of slave holdings (e.g. Charles Cotesworth Pickney-SC; George Mason-VA). Even Benjamin Franklin (PA) had freed his last slave only two years before the Convention began.

For Northerners, slavery was more focused on household slaves performing servant duties. This was not a world of large plantations that required vast cheap labor, so slaves represented a small percentage of those populations. Massachusetts had already moved to outlaw slavery in that state; other northern and middle states were moving towards that same end for either moral reasons or a lack of economic justification. (New York had the largest slave population in the northern region.)

From Maryland on down, however, the picture changed dramatically. This was plantation country, large farms that required large numbers of field workers to manage the crops. In the upper southern states, slaves accounted for perhaps 25-40% of

65

the population; in South Carolina and Georgia the percentage may have been closer to 50%, or even higher on the coastline plantations. The importation and use of slaves was also tied to the commercial ability to export the results of their labors. The upper southern states were moving towards more diversified crops than just their old standby of tobacco, and these mixed crops were requiring less slave labor to produce. But in South Carolina and Georgia, rice and indigo were the primary crops and economic base along the coastline plantations, and harvesting these crops was dirty and unhealthy work dependent upon slave labor. Given their major investment in buying slaves and the price they could bring in any resale, slaves represented property (if not a commodity) which counted as wealth to these large landowners.

Most of the crops produced by these southern slaves were destined for overseas exports, not just for local consumption. This further meant that for the large slave-holding states, non-interference in the buying / selling / holding of slaves was just one part of their economic well-being; an undisturbed export trade was the second important key to their economic success.

All of these issues had first surfaced early in the Convention's deliberations over the issue of representation in the new Congress. If "wealth" was to be the determining factor in allocating representation, then clearly the slaves – representing southern wealth – should count towards that calculation. And/or if population was to be the determinant, then it was clearly to the advantage of these southern states to include the slaves in that number – even if these same slaves had no citizenship rights whatsoever and were inherently assumed to be fully excluded from any constitutional recognition or participation. The northern states saw that a full count of slaves would dilute their potential congressional allocation, so they were equally vested in excluding slaves from the counting rules. The solution seen for this contentious dilemma came from a compromise introduced in mid-June by James Wilson (PA) supported by Charles Pickney (SC).

Borrowing from a taxation formula that had been attempted by the Confederation Congress several years previously, the final version of a calculation plan for representation stated that the number of representatives apportioned to each state "… shall be determined by adding to the whole Number of free Persons, including those bound to Service for a Term of Years [*i.e. indentured servants*], and excluding Indians not taxed, *three-fifths of all other Persons* [*i.e. slaves – emphasis added*]." By this compromise, all free white persons of both genders and all ages were to be included in the calculation of a citizen's right to governmental representation, but a significant proportion of the population would only be counted as 3/5^{ths} of a whole person, and not be otherwise entitled to the benefits of such representation.

Further, in the process of finalizing the draft of the Constitution, two other issues arose and were dealt with. One was the seemingly (and unseemly) unending continuation of the slave trade. Given the South's vested interest in the slave population and its effect on representation in the House, Northerners feared that unbridled continuation of the slave importation would continue to skew representation in favor of the southern states, even though it was being magnified by populations with no say in governance. So a push was made to end any future business in such importation. In response to South Carolina's and Georgia's threat to bolt the Convention over this issue, yet another compromise was reached: the importation of slaves would be left unchecked for now, to be halted after a "twenty year period" (i.e. in 1808); in turn the Southerners gave up opposition to giving the national government the power to regulate international trade collectively and on a simple majority vote rather than leaving each state to regulate individually (as was presently the case). The slaves currently in America and those imported until 1808, and the institution of slavery itself, would be left intact. A commitment to adopting a new Constitution, even if it might be a flawed one, took precedence over a blatant inconsistency in human rights. (As it turned out, the Northern fears of unbridled importation were quite justified. In the twenty year period before importation was eliminated, almost as many slaves were additionally imported than had been brought in during all the years up to that point.)

<u>The second issue was the legal affirmation of a status of bondage.</u> As a final statement on the matter of slavery, and the treatment of Negroes as "property" rather than human beings and citizens, and after the counting and importation issues had been worked through, Pierce Butler (SC) introduced a proposal that would expressly obligate the return of escaped slaves to their owners, no matter where such slaves may have been able to relocate themselves. Surprisingly, perhaps due to the delegates' exhaustion over the whole divisive issue of slavery, it passed unanimously without protest – virtually the only constitutional proposal to do so (except perhaps the proposal to end the Convention!).

The issue of slavery had provoked some emotional speeches at various times during the designing of the Constitution. But in the end, like the proceedings surrounding the writing of the Declaration of Independence, the delegates punted on the issue and eliminated any explicit language references to slavery or attempts to end the practice. While many delegates (some Southerners included) in both groups were opposed to slavery and thought it a "stain" on the documents and the whole nobility of the American cause, no one was willing to let this seemingly intractable issue be a deal-breaker that would separate the individual colonies/states and prevent their unanimous union. Times were changing: all of the northern and middle states were already in the process of prohibiting slavery in their borders in a "phasing out" approach. In Virginia, the demand for slaves was diminishing, but even George Washington and James Madison's personal feelings against slavery were not enough for them to disavow it and free their slaves; their personal fortunes were still deeply tied to it.

In spite of whatever moral outrage might be rising across the country at large in 1787, slavery was simply a generally accepted way of life. It was an institution that had been in place almost since the founding of Colonial America – and as we have seen, for thousands of years before and then still in place in other "civilized" parts of the world. Even those delegates who objected to slavery did not necessarily then equate that the Negro was equally competent with the white population; the Negro as inherently intellectually and morally inferior to the white, incapable of successfully intermingling with white persons, was the generally accepted view. The Northerners who objected to slavery were nowhere near as passionate about or committed to eliminating it as the Southerners of the Deep South were in defending it. The line in the sand drawn by South Carolina and Georgia was deemed a line not worth crossing.

Yet one cannot help feeling that most delegates knew that they had backed down on this issue. The fact that the word "slave" is nowhere mentioned expressly in the Constitution gives some hint as to how hard and purposefully they had to work to avoid calling attention to this lack of resolution. "All other persons" was the convenient and innocent-sounding euphemism to eliminate from political view perhaps 20% of the overall population of the United States. Yet it only postponed the reckoning to another day. Years of multiple laws, continuing instances of political brinkmanship, and major compromises attempting to prevent slavery, states' rights and economic differences from breaking apart the Union would ultimately prove futile. Over 600,000 American lives would be lost to finally settle the legal question of slavery as a result of the American Civil War (aka War Between the States) between 1861-1865. It would be followed by 100 more years of deep regional cultural division within the country, and our still continuing efforts to translate slave emancipation into true freedom and equality.

As if to acknowledge this great omission of action and of word, John Dickinson (DE) wrote privately:

"Acting before the World, What will be said of this new principle of founding a Right to govern Freemen on a power derived from Slaves, ... [who are] themselves incapable of governing yet giving to others what they have not. The omitting of the WORD [i.e. slave] will be regarded as an Endeavor to conceal a principle of which we are ashamed."[12]

The larger issue that arises from the protected debate regarding handling slavery in America was that it was really a debate about the more fundamental "equality" issue. Was "all men are created equal" to be simply nice sounding words, or a genuine article of faith and reality in America? Was slavery just another expression of the Founders' distrust of "the common man," albeit a more extreme distrust with respect to slaves? Enslavement of the African-American was a blatant example of a failure to extend equality to all Americans. *It portended a difficult and continual battle throughout our history to genuinely extend full freedom and rights to all Americans regardless of race, gender, or any other differentiating factors.* It is a battle that America still wrestles with today.

VIII. CONCLUDING THE CONVENTION BUSINESS

On Saturday, September 15, after months of debates, compromises, revisions and adjustments, George Washington was at last able to call the question regarding acceptance of a "final draft" of a new Constitution for the United States. James Madison recorded the result in a simple, declarative sentence:

> "On the question to agree to the Constitution as amended, all the States Ay."[1]

On Monday, after a day off from all of their intense final deliberations over the prior several weeks, 41 of the 55 delegates met together for the last time. For four months they had worked six days a week through endless hours of discussion, debate, intellectual reasoning, frustrations and challenges generating numerous compromises, resulting in no one getting everything they had wanted yet everyone getting something of worthwhile substance. For a few, partial victories were not enough; they had recognized that their positions were heading for defeat, so they had packed their bags and gone home before the Convention's business was even concluded.

This final session commenced with a word-by-word reading of the final draft of the Constitution, copies of which had been secretly prepared over the weekend by a local printer. The reading began with the short but important Preamble, principally the work of Gouverneur Morris (PA). The opening words famously read, "We, the People ..." In those first simple three words, the essence of four months' work was encapsulated. The new form of government being announced that day would not be a government

71

of kings, of divine right, of church, of nobility, or of state legislatures, but a government derived from and for all of the people (even if not everyone in attendance was confident in the ability of those people to actually run that government). This Constitution was being created "... in Order to form a more perfect Union"; perfection itself was deemed a goal not (yet) achievable, but achieving a major step forward towards perfecting the limitations of the Articles of Confederation was a worthy goal of accomplishment. Through that more perfect Union, the goal for the people was to "... establish Justice, insure domestic Tranquility, provide for the common defence, promote the general Welfare, and secure the Blessing of Liberty to ourselves and posterity ..." Justice, Tranquility, Defense, General Welfare, and the Blessings of Liberty – not a bad set of goals for any government, for any country.

William Jackson, the Convention's secretary, then read through all of the Articles contained within the Constitution. As they listened to the final words of the document, the delegates no doubt thought back to all of the difficult decisions they had made over the past four months, the deals that had been struck, the compromises agreed to in order to keep the Convention moving forward, even as failure continually loomed large. They may have also been struck by the simplicity of what they had wrought: four handwritten pages were all that it took to frame this government. Compared to the hundreds of pages that make up many of today's state constitutions, and the thousands of pages consumed in writing up a (frequently incomprehensible) national budget or law, the brevity yet effectiveness of their conclusions is striking in its brilliance. For this we owe a debt to the insightful Edmund Randolph (VA), a member of the Committee charged earlier with drafting this Constitution. It was his recommendation early on, adopted by the full Convention, that their Constitution be written based upon two key guidelines:

- *"to insert essential principle only,* lest the operations of government should be clogged by rendering those provisions permanent and unalterable, *which ought to be accommodated to times and events* (*italics added*); and

- *To use simple and precise language,* and general propositions, according to the example of the constitutions of the several states, for the construction of *a constitution necessarily differs from that of law."*[2] (*italics added*)

After this detailed reading, Benjamin Franklin gave a concluding address to the delegates (read by his Pennsylvania colleague James Wilson due to Franklin's ill health). Franklin had influenced little of the final substance of the Constitution. But at age 81 he was the recognized leading Founder and spirit in the room, a delegate without peer or questionable credentials or motivations. His life had encompassed the century of the 1700s, the century of growing up from English colonies into American states. His personal life was the prototypical American story of being born in poverty, making his own way and fortune, and achieving great recognition from his fellow Americans and the world for his accomplishments and statesmanship. He was now approaching the end of that storied life (he would die less than three years after the Convention ended); this Constitution would be his final contribution to his country. Appreciating the quality of the work produced, yet mindful of the specific concerns that plagued most of the delegates, and respectful of the dissent reflected in the absence of some of the delegates, Franklin sought to put their efforts into a perspective that could allow them to end on a positive note and bring them together in shared accomplishment. He stated that:

> "Mr. President, I confess that there are several parts of this constitution which I do not at present approve. But I am not sure I will never approve them. For having lived long, I have experienced many instances of being obliged by better

73

information or fuller consideration, to change opinions even on important subjects, which I once thought right, and found to be otherwise. It is therefore that the older I grow the more apt I am to doubt my own judgment and pay more respect to the judgment of others.

Most men indeed as well as most sects in religion think themselves in possession of all truth, and that wherever others differ from them it is so far error ... But though many private persons think almost as highly of their own infallibility as that of their sect, few express it so naturally as a certain French lady, who in a dispute with her sister, said, 'I don't know how it happens, Sister, but I meet with nobody but myself, that's always in the right.' In these sentiments, Sir, I agree to this Constitution with all its faults, if they are as such, because I think a general government necessary for us ... I doubt too whether any other Convention we can obtain may be able to make a better Constitution.

... Whenever you assemble a number of men to have the advantage of their joint wisdom, you inevitably assemble with those men all their prejudices, their passions, their errors of opinion, their local interests, and their selfish views. From such an assembly, can a perfect production be expected? ... It therefore astonishes me, Sir, to find this system [of government] approaching so near to perfection as it does; and I think it will astonish our enemies ...

... I consent, Sir, to this Constitution because I expect no better and because I am not sure that it is not the best. The opinions I have had of its errors, I sacrifice to the public good. I have never whispered a syllable of them abroad. Within these walls they were born, and here [my objections] shall die."

It is a sentiment and wisdom sorely needed again in this early 21st Century.

Having attempted to bring dissention over the document's details into a consensus of it as a whole, Franklin concluded by saying:

"Sir, I cannot help expressing a wish that every member of the Convention who may still have objections to it, would with me, on this occasion doubt a little bit of his own infallibility – and to make manifest our unanimity, put his name to this instrument."[3]

He then put forth a proposal (thought to have been actually drafted by Gouverneur Morris) that allowed for a face-saving step where such face-saving might be needed. The proposal requested that the document be signed reflecting the unanimous consent *of the states* (versus the delegates) present on that day. This narrow legalistic interpretation would then allow individual delegates to sign as a representative of their states, affirming only that their state's delegation had voted in favor of approval. Their signature would therefore not mean that the delegate was *personally* in favor of the document. It was a wording sleight-of-hand, admittedly. But it was another instance that reflected the importance the delegates felt about achieving their three main goals from this Convention: 1) to eliminate the Articles of Confederation that were seen as insufficient; 2) to replace them with a stronger national level of government; and 3) to have all the states on board in unanimous agreement, even if such unanimity took them down roads of difficult compromise on the details.

The proposal was adopted. (This approach would at least bring the signature of William Blount [NC] to the page, who otherwise was leaning towards not signing.)

A few final adjustments were made in the details of the articles (tinkering until the end!), and a few final speeches were given by both opposers and supporters. Then George Washington, as presiding officer of the convention, called for the act of signing. Washington signed first, ex officio as the presiding officer. Then, as was the custom, starting with northernmost New Hampshire and working their way geographically down to Georgia, the delegates approached the table and signed.

In the end, it was not a unanimous approval in spite of all the efforts to make it so. Eleven of the thirteen states approved the document. Rhode Island was still not present. New York had no quorum present, so even though technically his state had no vote and made no formal approval, Alexander Hamilton went ahead and signed the document anyway on New York's behalf. North Carolina's delegates originally rejected the final version, then changed and accepted it. Only three of Virginia's seven delegates would sign the document.

Three attending delegates refused to sign on that last day due to their misgivings in spite of Franklin's entreaties and wordplay: Edmund Randolph (VA); George Mason (VA); Elbridge Gerry (MA). One of the 14 delegates not in attendance, John Dickson (DE), gave George Read written instructions to sign on his behalf; four absent delegates were thought opposed to the Constitution; nine absent delegates were thought in favor of it. For a Convention seeking unanimity, 39 out of 55 votes and eleven of the thirteen states would have to do. For now. (See Appendix 1.)

With all the discussions ended, and with signing now complete, James Madison wrote his last, simple entry in his notes:

76

"The Constitution being signed by all the Members present except Mr. Randolph, Mr. Mason, and Mr. Gerry who declined giving it the sanction of their names, the Convention dissolved itself by an Adjournment sine die."[4]

Work complete, the delegates then did what many good Americans do on such an occasion: they ate and drank in celebration. George Washington wrote in his diary for that day:

"The business being closed, the members adjourned to City tavern, dined together and took a cordial leave of each other; after which I returned to my lodgings, did some business with, and received the papers from the Secretary of the Convention [i.e. William Jackson, the official record keeper], and retired to meditate on the momentous work which had been executed, after not less than five, and for a large part of the time, Six, and sometimes 7 hours sitting every day, except Sundays and the ten days of adjournment for more than four months."[5]

The story is told that shortly after the last session concluded, Benjamin Franklin was leaving the Pennsylvania State House when he encountered one Elizabeth Powel. Ms. Powel asked Dr. Franklin, "Well, Doctor, what have we got – a republic or a monarchy?" Franklin is said to have replied, "A republic, if you can keep it."[6] That is the challenge handed to each of us these many years and generations later by these 55 "plain, honest men": to show whether or not we are capable of Keeping It.

In his summary introduction to the publication of his "Journal of the Federal Convention," James Madison concluded his overall observations of the Convention's work, and the men who did that work, by saying 50 years later:

77

"But whatever may be the judgment pronounced on the competency of the architects of the Constitution, or whatever may be the destiny of the edifice prepared by them, I feel it a duty to express my profound and solemn conviction, derived from my intimate opportunity of observing and appreciating the views of the Convention, collectively and individually, that there was never an assembly of men, charged with a great and arduous task, who were more pure in their motives, or more exclusively or anxiously devoted to the object committed to them, than were the members of the Federal Convention of 1787, to the object of devising and proposing a constitutional system which should best supply the defects of that which it was to replace, and best secure the permanent liberty and happiness of their country."[7]

IX. ACCEPTANCE BY THE PEOPLE – JUST BARELY

The work of the Convention may have come to completion. But now the very hard work of getting each of the individual states and the general population on board would have to begin immediately. Timing and strategy would prove to be critical, given that adoption was by no means assured.

The truth is, this new Constitution that we prize so much today *came remarkably close to never being accepted.* There were many strong objections to this new central power being created over the previous sovereignty of each state. Many of those objections to this new form of government are still heard as the basis of many debates today. So we need to look closely at how narrowly the Constitution was ultimately accepted, and listen to the original voices of argument that we still hear echoed today.

The Convention had preempted some of that anticipated difficulty by including within the Constitution itself the formula and method for its adoption. The Confederation Congress, in its original charge to the convention, had expected that the delegates would develop their proposed amendments and report them back to the Congress for further action. Given that the Convention ultimately scraped the Confederation and its Congress altogether, they came up instead with a different approach. The prevailing thought became that, since this would be a government "Of the People" and not "of the states," then this Constitution needed to be accepted or rejected by the people who would be governed by its terms. The means to accomplish that was not to leave the decision to the Confederation Congress (where all decisions required unanimous approval – an unlikely outcome in this case) or to the

79

state legislatures who had a primary interest in self-preservation. Rather, it was decided to use new conventions called within each state, with the singular purpose to decide yea or nay on this proposed Constitution, without making any amendments thereto, with the delegates to these ratification conventions being elected directly by the people. It was a gutsy call for those days and times. But Nathaniel Gorham (MA) observed that "Men chosen by the people for the particular purpose, will discuss the subject more candidly than members of the legislature who are to lose power which is to be given up to the general government."[1] He was proven to be very right in his analysis.

In another slap to the Confederation structure, it was also determined that 2/3^{rds} of any combination of the states (i.e. any nine states) would be sufficient for the Constitution to go into effect. After months of haggling over issues of representation and the conflicts and protections of big-state versus small-state interests, the process for ratification had the effect of going back to the usual concept of equal votes regardless of size, wealth or power (making the adoption process all the more interesting as things turned out).

As the Constitutional Convention wrapped up as of September 17, the delegates headed either home or to their seats in the Confederation Congress to begin the ratification battle. Only three days later, on September 20, the document was formally reported back and presented to the Congress. On the 26th, discussion on its contents began. It was a lop-sided discussion, because 18 of the Congress' 33 delegates had served as Convention delegates; most all of those 18, together with their allies, were highly committed to its adoption. So after only two days of debate, on September 28th the Congress resolved that "Having received the report from the Convention lately assembled in Philadelphia, Resolved Unanimously that the said report, together with the resolutions and letter accompanying the same, be transmitted to the several state legislatures."[2] And so the ratification battle moved quickly to the thirteen individual states.

Each of those thirteen battles can easily be its own separate and interesting story. Stories of political intrigue, strategy, political and governance differences, cast of characters and how they maneuvered, as each state handled the question differently under the same guidelines that had been set up.

For the "Federalists" who supported the Constitution, they had the advantage of being better skilled in defending the provisions of the Constitution having spent months already debating it at every level of detail. The smaller states – once the representation issue had been resolved – saw their economic future better served by having consistent trade laws in place across the Union, rather than dictated by the few wealthy states. There were also still the increasing calls for something different than the Confederation to be put into place, and the Federalists had *a plan* on the table ready to go, attached with the great weight of endorsement by Washington and Franklin (even though neither would actively campaign for it). They were organized with a game plan: the vote on the Constitution would be straight up or down, yea or nay; no revisions, no amendments; get on board or get left behind; you may quibble on some details, but do you really want to be left out and come away with nothing? These Federalists had a certain sense of momentum and enthusiasm driving their cause, and they were fully prepared to ride it.

For the "Anti-federalists," they had left the Convention in the minority. (Indeed, some had missed much of the later discussions and would therefore prove to be less skilled in the upcoming debates in the state conventions). Their objections, genuinely felt, generally centered around the diminution of the powers and primacy of the states; the loss of the ideal that state governments are the most closely connected to the people; the increase in power seen to be accumulating in the national government; the fear of

81

"the President" paving the way for a future monarchy; and the perceived lack of input from the common people versus the elite, wealthy delegates (this "class" argument would be fully exploited in some of the state debates). In the background, of course, was the recent Revolution and the blood expended to throw off a distant, powerful English government in favor of individual freedom. It would take a great leap of faith, impossible for some, to move from revolutionary fervor to a theoretical, unproven, constitutional national government, even if it was a "federal" one. But time would be short for them to organize, and they had no alternative constitution to offer. *Just saying "no" without offering a tangible, viable alternative does not usually buy you support from the American people.*

The sequential battle for ratification would move one state at a time across the union, with some states delaying action on the issue. (This sequence and delay would prove to work to the Federalists' advantage.) It was easy for Pennsylvania to be the first to take up the issue. The Constitutional Convention had been held in its State House, and news of its results traveled fast throughout Philadelphia. But time was short because the Pennsylvania legislature was slated to adjourn in less than two weeks hence. So even before they got official word from the Confederation Congress meeting in New York City, the Pennsylvania legislature worked out the ground rules to quickly call its ratifying convention. Congress' official word to the Pennsylvania legislature came on the 28th, but the Anti-federalist legislators boycotted the session in order to prevent a quorum. So the Federalists hired a group of men to go out and find some of the boycotting legislators and bring them back into the Assembly. Two were so found, dragged back, and forcibly inserted into their chairs. The vote to call the ratification convention thereby passed a few hours short of adjournment!

And so Pennsylvania began its convention on November 21st following the people's election of their delegates. The Federalists held a 2:1 majority of these delegates, supported mainly by both educated and working-class Philadelphians. It was a free-wheeling discussion, open to the public to attend and listen to the seemingly unending debates that went on for weeks. But the extended time was important – especially given the "class" charge – so that all participants could have their say, no matter how many times it might take to say it. James Wilson, a Constitutional Convention delegate, led the charge for the Federalists. He argued that it was not simply a choice to be made between having a single, comprehensive national government versus "thirteen separate, independent commonwealths." Rather there was this new option being offered for "... a comprehensive Federal Republic." In this new Federal Republic, authority:

> "... remains and flourishes with the people ... That the supreme power, therefore, should be vested in the people, is in my judgment the great panacea of human politics. It is a power paramount to every constitution, inalienable in its nature, and indefinite in its extent ... [assessing] the streams of power that appear through this great and comprehensive plan, we shall be able to trace them to one great and noble source, THE PEOPLE."[3]

When the time finally came to vote on December 12th, ratification passed along the original pro/against lines – 46 for, 23 against. After all the hours of debate, few if any minds had been changed. *But the precedent of allowing all to speak, to voice their concerns, was politically key to this convention and many of the conventions to come.* The next day, after a victory procession through the streets of Philadelphia and a public reading of the ratification resolution, the parade marched to Epple's Tavern for – what else – a drink in self-congratulations for what they had accomplished.

If Pennsylvania was the first out the door towards ratification, they would not be the first to the finish line. Delaware started second, holding its convention starting December 2nd. Under the tight control of George Read and John Dickinson, Delaware's two delegates to the Constitutional Convention, Delaware unanimously voted 30 to 0 for ratification on December 7th. It was five days ahead of Pennsylvania, and gave Delaware perpetual bragging rights as "The First State."

Close on their heels was New Jersey. That ratifying convention met, and in only one week on December 16th it also voted unanimously 38 to 0 for ratification. Once Pennsylvania was seen as going for ratification, the small neighboring states of Delaware and New Jersey had opted not to be left behind. Given these quick actions, within only three months of its signing by the Constitutional Convention three states were on board with the new Constitution. The momentum was now indeed on the Federalists' side; it would be on the shoulders of the Anti-federalists to try to stop it.

Moving into 1788, Georgia, one of the weaker states needing economic and trade protection for its agriculture, and physical protection against the Spanish in Florida as well as its resident Indians, voted unanimously 26 to 0 for ratification on January 2nd. Four states were now on board.

Next came Connecticut. Similar to what happened in New Jersey, Connecticut's Constitutional Convention delegates (Roger Sherman, Oliver Ellsworth, and William Johnson) led the charge. They managed the ratifying convention and wrote extensive articles (especially Ellsworth) in support of the proposal. On January 4th, the convention voted 128 to 40 for ratification. Five states were now on board.

These votes proved to be the easier battles. Next in order would come the problem states, the large and wealthier states long accustomed to being the political powers within the Union. Massachusetts started meeting on January 9th, 1788. It had chosen

355 delegates to its ratifying convention, accompanied by hundreds of spectators to listen to the debates. Given its long tradition of town meetings and high political engagement by its citizens, and its long history of political leadership and independence, interest in the constitutional question and the protection of Massachusetts' political and economic independence was very high within the state.

The complication was that both John Hancock and Samuel Adams, two renowned and trusted names from the Revolution, started out as skeptical towards the whole constitutional enterprise. Elbridge Gerry, one of the Constitutional Convention delegates from Massachusetts, had been highly opposed to this Constitution during the Convention debates and was ready to continue that personal fight into this ratifying convention. But fortunately Gerry would be limited to not speaking at this gathering, only providing written responses to questions – effectively limiting if not shutting him out of the floor debate.

The basic fight that emerged turned on the "class" issue: the perception that this Constitution was the work of (according to participant Amos Singletary) "these lawyers, and men of learning, and moneyed men, that talk so finely, and gloss over matters so smoothly to make us poor little people swallow down the pill."[4] Given this broad-based sentiment, the Federalists agreed to a full and open public discussion to assure that "the common man" would be heard. Then they also took the strategically dangerous step of agreeing that potential <u>future</u> amendments to the Constitution could be discussed as long as they did not become *preconditions* to ratification. This decision put the "yea or nay unaltered" strategy at risk of starting an avalanche of proposed changes, revisitations and renegotiations of the decisions already discussed and made at the Constitutional Convention. But in the end it would prove to be a saving tactic – for Massachusetts as well as some of the other remaining states. The ability to offer up some proposed amendments to this Constitution for early consideration in the first Congress served to assuage Hancock and Adams in spite of their underlying hesitancies. On February 6th, following a speech by Hancock urging ratification along with nine proposed amendments thereto, the convention voted 187 to 168 for ratification. It was the closest vote to date, but the Constitution had prevailed. <u>Six</u> states were now on board. Voting now headed to the southern states.

There was one other action coming out of the Massachusetts debates that merits special mention. At the conclusion of the very close vote, which came following hard-fought arguments of deep beliefs from good, principled people on both sides, Benjamin Swain spoke to the convention regarding his feelings on being on the losing side.

> Swain told the other participants that "the Constitution had had a fair trial and there had not … been any undue influence exercised to obtain the vote in its favor; that many doubts which lay on his mind had been removed," and that, although he was in the minority, "he should support the Constitution as cheerfully and as heartily as though he had voted on the other side of the question."[5] It was a position not just of magnanimity, but it was also a principle that is essential for democratic government to succeed: *after a fair hearing and honest vote, the decision is thereby made and all must come together to make the decision work.*

In Maryland, there was wide-spread public support for the Constitution, and once again the Federalists were in firm control of the convention. On April 26th, the convention voted 63 to 11 for ratification. <u>Seven</u> states were now on board.

The South Carolina convention convened in May. As in Delaware and Connecticut, that state's Constitutional Convention delegates

(Charles Pickney, Charles Cotesworth Pickney, and John Rutledge) shepherded the process. Nearly one-third of the delegates were family relatives, and the low-country plantation people who shared common interests of large wealth dominated the attendees. The continuation of slavery was the biggest overall concern, just as it had been represented by that state's Convention delegates. But the Pickneys and Rutledge were able to convince these participants that, based upon the cooperation they had received from the northern delegates at the Convention, their interest had been (and would be) protected. On May 23rd, the convention voted 149 to 73 for ratification. Eight states were now on board.

New Hampshire, famously always the contrarian going its own way, had originally met on February 13th with 113 participants attending. After ten days of debate, the Federalists were facing likely defeat. So they moved to adjourn until further notice, hoping that the delegation would come around after more states had gotten on board. The second time they tried, with Massachusetts and Maryland now on board, they were successful, albeit still with great resistance showing. On June 21st, the convention finally voted 57 to 47 for ratification. Nine states, the minimum required, were now on board! And so ratification had been technically achieved, and the new Constitution and government of the United States came into being on that date of June 21, 1788. The reluctant state had become the enabling state. But two big and important states (Virginia and New York) had not yet been heard from. As a practical matter their agreement would also be needed for a true "United States" to be a successful reality.

So the critical battle now moved to Virginia, starting on June 2nd. With eight states known to be already on board as Virginia began its discussions, saying "no" would be a tough decision and going against the unanimous tide to date. But as the most populous and wealthiest state, with the likely first President already presumed to come from their ranks (George Washington), if Virginia opted to decline it had the potential to undermine all the progress made to date. Getting their assent was crucial, and by no means was a yes vote assured.

Patrick Henry was the most admired and powerful politician in the state. He was a full believer in the sanctimony and primacy of Virginia above all other states, an opinion shared by many of his Virginia countrymen. He made up his mind early on to be unalterably opposed to this Constitution. George Mason, like Elbridge Gerry in Massachusetts, was a Convention delegate greatly opposed to the Constitution and was working insistently and consistently to spread his objections throughout the ratifying convention. It would be touch and go all through the debates, with the potential result unknown. James Madison, the leader of the Federalist participants, observed that "the business is in the most ticklish state that can be imagined. The majority will certainly be small on whatever side it may finally lie; and I dare not encourage much expectation that it will be on the favorable side."[6] The eastern coastal Virginia participants were generally disposed in favor of the Constitution; the middle and backcountry Virginians were opposed; and the western Virginians (now Kentucky) were generally unknown in their potential leanings.

In the debates, Mason's continued rantings against the Constitution and his extended debates over the smallest of details became so extreme that even his potential allies began to turn against him. Henry, while quite eloquent at times in promoting the parochial view of Virginia's superior greatness over the other states, took to the tactic of demanding amendments (as many as 40 at one point!) to be made in the Constitution as a *precondition* for ratification. To counter these various forms of resistance, Madison served as an effective debater given all his work during the Convention debates; he was well-prepared and well-versed in the many arguments offered. In the meantime, Washington (who chose not to attend the ratifying convention) and Madison had been quietly working in the background on Edmund Randolph, a Convention delegate who had chosen not to sign the Constitution because of his great concerns over the creation of too much central government. Their efforts paid off when Randolph, sensing the direction of history, rose in his closing speech to the convention and stated:

> "I went to the federal Convention with the strongest affection for the Union; ... I acted there in full conformity with this affection; ... I refused to subscribe, because I had, as I still have, objections to this Constitution, and wished a free inquiry into its merits; [but] the accession of eight states reduced our deliberations into the single question of Union or no Union."[7]

Unlike Patrick Henry, Randolph had come to believe that there would be no real future for Virginia outside of the new Union. And with eight states having already voted yes, the direction was clear. Regardless of the detailed concerns, Virginia needed to be included and seek out its future within the new structure. Not knowing that New Hampshire had already become the 9th state to ratify four days previously, on June 25th the convention narrowly voted 89 to 79 for ratification. Ten states were now on board, but Virginia was the biggest prize.

Patrick Henry, the famous statesman, (likely unknowingly) followed the lead of Benjamin Swain, the commoner from Massachusetts, in being conciliatory to the outcome. Following the vote and the defeat of his position, he promised that "I will be a peaceable citizen. My head, my hand, and my heart, shall be at liberty to retrieve the loss of liberty and remove the defects of that system in a constitutional way."[8] He would continue to work to correct this "defective Constitution," but he would do so in a legal way through the constitutional amendment process.

That left the next big prize remaining: New York. The Federalists had their working majority sufficient to form the new government.

But unanimity was still the larger prize, so getting New York into the fold was still a big goal. New Yorkers were as resistant as the Virginians: two of the three delegates to the Constitutional Convention had packed up and left due to their objections, depriving New York of any official voice in those proceedings; 46 of the 65 ratifying convention participants now gathered were initially opposed. Governor George Clinton and the two New York dissenting delegates, Robert Yates and John Lansing, would lead the opposition here. They had hoped Virginia's rejection would strengthen their case, but having lost that battle and with ten states already assenting, the cause of rejection was greatly against them. Nevertheless, they would have their say regardless of the decisions of others.

The debates went on for weeks, fed and influenced by the publication in the New York newspapers of a series of articles under the heading of "The Federalist." These papers explained and advocated at length the meaning of the Constitution's words, the necessity of the provisions, the benefits of the federal structure, and the legal, moral and practical basis for adopting this Constitution. The 85 articles were written by John Jay, Alexander Hamilton (primarily), and James Madison. They each wrote separately under the one pseudonym "Publicus," uncoordinated with each other, and cranked out in a hurry from October 1787 until May 1788, all in order to influence the public and the various convention debates. The writings ultimately spread like wildfire to the public, reaching audiences all up and down the union beyond New York. If Thomas Paine's *Common Sense* was the literary argument for the Revolution, The Federalist could be seen as the literary argument for the Constitution, with another tip of the hat to Johannes Gutenberg's most important printing press. Even today, The Federalist remains as one of the best explanations for modern jurists as to the why and wherefore reasonings underlying the Constitution.

Ultimately, given the reality of their situation being near the end of the voting line, most delegates were not willing to reject the Constitution outright. Like Massachusetts and Virginia before them, they therefore put their dissenting energies into the idea of proposing constitutional amendments. After sorting through all manner of potential amendments to be offered up, on July 25th the convention narrowly voted 30 to 27 for ratification. New York continued its reputation of being one of the most reluctant of the states: in the writing of the Declaration of Independence; in the designing of the Constitution of the United States; and now in the ratification of that Constitution. (New York would subsequently miss out in participating in the first Electoral College's unanimous vote for President George Washington due to deadlocking in selecting its eight delegates!) It would have taken only two people to have swung their state to the negative side. Regardless, eleven states were now on board, including the big fishes of Massachusetts, Virginia, and New York.

At this point, it remained only to round up the outliers. North Carolina's ratifying convention convened on July 21st, fully knowing that the decision had already been made by the other states. But like New York, they chose to also make their voices heard regardless, as the Anti-federalists had a 2:1 majority in this convention. The debates got very heated and even personal at times. In this body, the dominant issue was that the Constitutional Convention had exceeded their authority well beyond their original charge by scrapping the Articles of Confederation. That, coupled with a high distrust of any centralized government, caused them to initially reject the constitution on August 2nd by a vote of 184 to 83. But they also proposed 46 amendments that, if adopted, might cause them to come around. It was the closest thing to *preconditioned* amendments that had been attempted by any of the ratifying conventions, even though others might have liked to have done so. As the newly-authorized government began to form, they essentially chose to ignore North Carolina and their objections. The federal government commenced operations and elected their first congressmen and president, and over time the enthusiasm of the North Carolinians for opposition wore out. On November 12, 1789, almost 16 months after New York's vote, eight months after the opening of the first Congress, and seven months after Washington's inauguration as the first President, North Carolina voted 194 to 77 for ratification. <u>Twelve</u> states were now on board.

That left Rhode Island the sole remaining state, ever protective of its self interest. Rhode Island was like the littlest kid in a playground filled with bigger, tougher and wealthier kids, yet constantly wagging its small finger at everyone in order to assert its independence. Rhode Island had skipped the Constitutional Convention entirely. Then it refused the Confederation Congress' request to call a ratifying convention to consider the new Constitution. Instead, each of their local town meetings was asked to debate the question of ratification. Based upon that popular voting tally, Rhode Islanders rejected the Constitution by an official vote of 2708 to 235. (But at least it was the only fully democratic voting by the people at large on the question!) So Rhode Island chose to sit out any meaningful participation or influence on this question of ratification. Finally, over six months after North Carolina had finally given up the fight, Rhode Island chose to join its Revolutionary compatriots. Life, and America, was moving on. On May 29, 1790, Rhode Island just barely voted 34 to 32 for adoption – fighting, kicking and screaming, even to the end. All <u>thirteen</u> states were now on board.

As said at the outset of this chapter, acceptance of the Constitution was anything but universal by our founding ancestors. Some staunch supporters of the Revolution were also just as staunch objectors to this new government. As summarized below, the smaller, less wealthy statues saw the Constitution as a reasonable protection for their interests and supported it strongly. The larger, more prosperous states accustomed to independent leadership accepted the Constitution by only the narrowest of margins. And three states initially rejected it altogether. But in the end, each state saw the country's larger direction and future, accepted the results, and came together as one united whole. *Even though this new government would be continually examined and tested and adjusted – most famously by the American Civil War / War Between The States – Americans' respect for the law and governmental process embodied in that Constitution remains firm and supreme.*

STATE VOTING ON ADOPTING THE CONSTITUTION

STATE	YEAS	NAYS	%
Small States:			
Delaware	30	0	100
New Jersey	38	0	100
Georgia	26	0	100
Connecticut	128	40	76
Maryland	63	11	85
Large and Wealthy States:			
Pennsylvania	46	23	67
Massachusetts	187	168	53
South Carolina	149	73	67
Virginia	89	79	53
New York	30	27	53
States Accepting After Initially Rejecting:			
New Hampshire	57	47	55
North Carolina	194	77	72
Rhode Island	34	32	52

The Constitution of the United States and the new form of government that it created was sufficiently ratified on June 21, 1788. It took substance on March 4, 1789 with the opening of the first Congress, was installed on April 29, 1789 with George Washington's inauguration as the first President, and was made whole on May 29, 1790 with the 13th state's final ratification. It had taken almost 200 years for America to move from its first permanent colonial English settlement in Jamestown to become a new, independent nation with an unknown and untried democratic / republican / federal form of government. "If," as Benjamin Franklin had said, "you can keep it."

X. UNFINISHED BUSINESS: THE BILL OF RIGHTS

Ratification done, there was now one additional piece of unfinished constitutional business to be taken care of. During the ratification debates of several states, the fact that the Constitution contained no Bill of Rights had generated much negativism towards the proposal. Specifically in Massachusetts, Virginia and New York where anti-Constitution sentiment ran high, the absence of such enumerated safeguards almost sank the ratification debates into defeat. Thomas Jefferson, no admirer of any big-styled government, decried the absence of a Bill of Rights after he first read the proposed Constitution. He would publicly support ratification despite his many misgivings, but preferred that "I equally wish that the four latest [state ratifying] conventions ... may refuse to accede to it, till a declaration of rights is annexed."[1] Hence the tactical offer had been made to allow the state conventions to suggest potential amendments (though not require them as a precondition to ratification). Now the newly ratified government needed to make good on that offer.

A Bill of Rights attached to the Constitution had a long historical precedence in the minds of many of the new Americans. Looking all the way back to the 1200s, the Magna Carta was the first written document putting some small limits on what had been the absolute power of the English King. Even though such limits were mainly focused towards protecting the rights of only a small group – the noblemen – it was a first step. The Magna Carta in turn served as the historical precedent for the Bill of Rights of 1689 following England's Grand Revolution of 1688-89. This declaration expressly enumerated the rights which James I had violated (and hence were the basis for removing him as king), and then specified certain rights of Parliament and the English citizen which the King could not violate. William of Orange and Mary II's joint acceptance of this Bill of Rights as a precondition to assuming the English throne bound all future kings to this Bill and assured its permanency.

There were additional precedents for written statements on the rights entitled to by the common citizen. King William's Toleration Act of 1689 went even further in pronouncing religious tolerance for all those believers in the Christian trinity who chose to worship outside the established Church of England (Anglican). In America, the Rhode Island colony founded by Roger Williams in 1636 was unique in its declaration of religious freedom: the right to follow one's own religious conscience; the absence of interference in that right by government – the foundation of the doctrine for separation of church and state. Rhode Island's provision for religious freedom (as well as democratic rule) was endorsed in its permanent royal charter subsequently granted by Charles II, even though England at that time was very strict in its requirements for religious conformity by the Church of England. Given Rhode Island's protection of religious freedom, Quakers, Jews, and Anabaptists had flocked to the colony. Similarly, Maryland had passed its Toleration Act in 1649 guaranteeing religious toleration, but only to those religions that believed in the concept of the Trinity; death was prescribed for non-believers, so it was a more limited form of toleration than in Rhode Island. In 1779, Thomas Jefferson had drafted a bill regarding religious freedom that in 1786 was adopted by the Virginia legislature as An Act for Establishing Religious Freedom.

Given these and other movements towards formally legalized guarantees of individual rights, the drive to include such statements as part of the formation of governmental entities was well rooted in America by the late 1700s. George Mason had written a "Declaration of Rights," adopted on June 12, 1776, for incorporation in Virginia's first state constitution. Some of

96

Mason's words and ideas (e.g. "...All men are by nature equally free and independent and have certain inherent rights," and "... enjoyment of life and liberty") had found their way into Thomas Jefferson's Declaration of Independence. Virginia's Declaration served as a model for a similar document adopted by Pennsylvania on August 16, 1776, for its state constitution. By the time of the Constitutional Convention, eight of the states had included some form of Declaration of Rights into their constitutions.

Given all of this background and precedence, it is all the more surprising that such a similar statement did not come out of the Constitutional Convention. In fact, such an idea was barely even considered. George Mason had proposed such an inclusion in the waning days of the Convention, reflecting his growing concern about the increasing power being given to the new central government (and perhaps reflecting his own experience – and pride – in authoring the Virginia Declaration of Rights). Amazingly in retrospect, such an idea had gone nowhere with the Convention delegates. The reasons given were generally that such a statement of state or individual rights was unnecessary. The Constitution only granted powers to the central government that were specifically stated, so trying to define all those powers *not* given to them was unnecessary; what all would have to be included, and where would you end such a detailed listing? Alexander Hamilton (NY) said later in his Federalist Papers writings, "Why declare that things shall not be done which there is no power in Congress to do?"[2] James Wilson (PA), with James Madison's (VA) support, went further to ask "Who will be bold enough to undertake to enumerate all the rights of the people? And when the attempt to enumerate them is made, it must be remembered that if the enumeration is not complete, everything not expressly mentioned will be presumed to be purposely omitted."[3] Besides, most of the state governments already had such declarations in their constitutions, and these state declarations would thereby protect the people. Some argued that the Constitution's Preamble stated that this government came from "We the People ...," so by definition the people retained their rights; no more was felt needed to be said.

What is far more likely than these legalistic arguments is that, by September 12th, a more practical (and human) issue was at hand: the goal of adjournment after long months of hard debate. The Convention's work was almost done. Words and Provisions were in the process of being fine-tuned towards completion. Next to no one wanted to start up a whole new topic of discussion which, given the Convention's history of contentiousness on each and every item, would likely be yet another long round of debate on wording and content – in spite of Mason's assurance that such a Bill could be written "in just a few hours." So with hardly a murmur of dissent, the Convention voted unanimously against writing and including such a Bill of Rights into the Constitution. As we saw, such an ill-considered omission would later serve as a major stumbling block in some of the key states. Thomas Jefferson was horrified to discover that no such protections were attached to the Constitution. He spoke for many when he wrote to James Madison, "Let me add that a bill of rights is what the people are entitled to against every government on earth, general or particular, and what no just government should refuse or rest on inference."[4]

Promises made must be promises delivered. As an early order of business in the first United States Congress, James Madison made good on his word in spite of his previous objections stated at the Convention. He introduced into that Congress a Resolution for the first 12 proposed Amendments to the Constitution, following the process provided for in that Constitution. They were offered, according to the Preamble of the Resolution, "… as extending the ground of public confidence in the Government, [in order to] best ensure the beneficent ends of its institution." His proposal drew heavily from George Mason's Declaration of Rights for Virginia, likely providing some delayed satisfaction and recognition to Mason given his refusal to sign the Constitution due to this omission.   Congress passed the proposed amendments on September 25th, 1789. The required 3/4-majority of states failed to accept the first two amendments, but formally accepted numbers 3-12 two years later on December 15, 1791.   It is these ten Amendments that make up the American Bill of Rights.

The Declaration of Independence defined our aspirations as a people and a country, and substantiated the basis for our separation from England and its King in order to run our own affairs. The Constitution created a pragmatic framework of rules and structures for managing a unified country of 13 previously independent states. But it is the Bill of Rights that draws a line in the sand that government dares not cross, a line that says there are some rights which are inherent in being an American. These enumerated rights are not to be taken away or circumvented under any circumstances by our national government. It is here where most Americans form their beliefs regarding American government: freedom to practice the religion of individual choice without government interference or favoritism; freedom of speech and the press, regardless of how unpopular or controversial the speech may be; the guarantee of prompt trials by laws and juries in public, versus secret trials on the whim of kings; and protection against unreasonable search and self-incrimination, cruel punishment and torture, or taking one's property without due process. These and other guaranteed rights had been taking shape for centuries, but came to full fruition in America's Bill of Rights, inseparable from the Constitution to which it was attached, and therefore permanently incumbent on the government established thereby to enforce and protect. They are the constitutional substance of people's "inalienable rights" referenced in Thomas Jefferson's Declaration of Independence.

It had taken just over 180 of America's first years.   But the working tools needed were now finally in place. Ben Franklin questioned whether we would be able to keep the Republic that had been given to us. The larger question for us to answer is whether we will be able to fulfill civilization's Purpose for which these tools, our Union and Republic, and America itself, was created.

XI. ACCOMPLISHMENT AND EXPECTATIONS

"This country and this people seem to have been made for each other."[1]
John Jay, *Federalist Papers*

America began its infancy in 1607, moved through its childhood until the end of that century, worked through its adolescence until 1775, and became a learned young adult in 1788 ready to take on the responsibilities of full adulthood. The many colonists who inhabited this country during these formative years passed on a legacy of character and expectations for all subsequent generations to work within. They went about their daily lives and the mundane work of living, surviving, providing for, creating, community-building, and ultimately dying as all people do. But many nevertheless intuitively felt that they were part of something different, something previously unknown in humankind's experience, something better, and they expected to pass on   that "something different" to their children and their children's children thereafter. Some would ascribe it all to Divine Intervention, God's handiwork guiding their direction and bringing them to this better place. Others would simply credit it with the flowering of humankind within a growing Age of Reason. And others, consumed with the difficult struggle for life within the backwood forests, would simply feel that they were seeking to improve their lot in life, and to gain an even better one for their children, and America was the place where that betterment could happen.

Winning the Revolutionary War with England was not easy. There was a great loss of life; families and friendships were pulled apart by conflicting allegiances; many homes and fortunes were destroyed; fear over an unpredictable outcome was always present. Once that war was won, it was not a victory to be taken lightly. Its rewards, so easily taken for granted, would demand continual vigilance; the goals, so easily lost by apathy, would require continual protection; the frailties of human character, ever gnawing on the strengths of human possibility, would require continual ethical reinforcement. The American victory could be fleeting, like so much of the European experience. Yet it could be lasting, like no other experience before it. But to be lasting, the future guardians – ourselves – need to fully and clearly understand the treasure being stored within the American story and behind its Constitutional walls so that our actions will be consistent with the expectations of its benefactors. So let us ensure that we fully and clearly understand the expectations upon us.

XII. THE TRUTHS OF THE CONSTITUTIONAL AGREEMENT

There is no question that the American Revolutionary / Founding period of 1775→1788 was one of the greatest flowerings of intellectual and creative thought in world history. The result was a statement of vision regarding the inherent rights of humankind and the framework of a mechanism for fulfilling that vision, brought about by an extraordinary coming together of the right people at the right moment. The results of their work have stood for over 200 subsequent years, and have ever since served as a model – if not in detailed form at least in ideal – for governance changes across the world.

We rightly respect the labors and outcomes of these Founders. But as we speak of them and work with their products, our high admiration often clouds our rightful understanding of them and the outcomes they gave to us. It is not enough to simply read their literal words on the parchment; it is also necessary that we understand how those words came about in the context of their times and circumstances, else we miss the true meaning and significance of their work. That has been the purpose of this narrative – to establish a fuller context for understanding. In that spirit, let us examine some of our more important impressions and subject them to the larger context that we have explored.

THE Founding Fathers – Individuals, not Unanimity

The cause of American independence, and the intention and meaning of the Constitution, were never agreed to by all Americans. There were many disagreements about the particular provisions of the Constitution, but in the end, near-unanimity

103

about the Constitution <u>as a whole</u> was accepted as the rule of the land.

The biggest mistake we make in our view of our Founding Fathers is that we treat them as a collective "they," being all of one unified mind "They said this"; "they believed that"; "they intended this." Such a view is a colossal misunderstanding on our part. The one theme that emerges from the story of those times is that these Founding Fathers – like Americans still today – had major disagreements about the direction of the country and how to govern it. Perhaps half of the country opposed the Revolution and preferred retaining our ties to England; we often fought among ourselves as much as against the English army. We very nearly lost the Revolutionary War, and likely would have had not France intervened on our side.

Following that war for independence, there were many governmental leaders who were perfectly happy with the Articles of Confederation and the severe limits it placed on that Congress, leaving the thirteen states independent and all-powerful. When the delegates convened in Philadelphia for the Constitutional Convention, some of them were aghast that a wholly new constitution was even being proposed versus some individual fine-tuning amendments to the Articles of Confederation. Creating our Constitution provoked major disagreements among those delegates; no one came out with everything they wanted, and nearly all expressed misgivings about some provision or another. George Washington expressed the prevailing view of most delegates when he wrote to Patrick Henry on the eve of Virginia's ratifying convention, "I wish the Constitution which is offered, had been made more perfect; but I sincerely believe it is the best that could be obtained at this time. And, as a constitutional door is opened for amendment hereafter, the adoption of it, under the present circumstances of the Union, is in my opinion desirable."[1]

James Madison may legitimately be called the Father of the Constitution, but the Constitution that emerged was significantly different than his original draft after all the bargaining and voting was finished. In conversations and writings years later, Madison expressed various misgivings about how power had been distributed to and within the federal government, even as he continued to express admiration for the overall work done by the delegates. When they were done, none of the delegates could claim to really know what the words truly meant or how it would all work in the day-to-day; the drive to agreement often overshadowed the substance of the meaning. The arguments over the *interpretation* of the Constitution's words continued as the delegates were going out the Convention door, reemerged with the first convening of the government, and continue to this day.

Today's arguments about the appropriate powers for the federal government are simply continuing echoes of the original Philadelphia debates. And as we also saw, when the people had the opportunity to speak on the matter, the Constitution barely survived votes for ratification in several key states. So it is silly in today's debates to speak that "the Founders thought thus." We must first ask "Which founder? On what topic? And what did other Founders think?" When it comes to what the Founders believed, there is no collective "They." Today's politicians who claim to speak for these men should immediately be held suspect.

Compromise
The Founders established by their own actions that our government works only if people of myriad beliefs come together to find the best possible solution for all.

If there is one primary precedent that arises out of the creation of the Constitution, it is that our nation was founded on a principle of compromise. Compromise was at the heart of the ongoing debates about every detail; compromise is built into the very structure and fabric of our Constitution and the government structures it created. The one overriding characteristic of Americans is a broad diversity of opinion and personal goals. So in a self-governing democracy, that diversity must find a way to yield to working agreements, else we are left with anarchy and a non-functioning government of only "*some* of the people" rather than "*We* the People." The American nation and its government were designed specifically so as to prevent absolutism in favor of "a middle way." A House of Representatives (the people at large), a Senate (the individual states), and a President (the Nation) must ultimately come together and resolve their differences before any monies are spent or any law is passed.

As Benjamin Franklin (PA) observed during the Convention, "When a broad table is to be made, and the edges of the planks do not fit, the artist takes a little from both, and makes a good joint. In a like manner here both sides must part with some of their demands in order that they may join in some accommodating proportion."[2]

It was only through compromise that we have a Constitution; it is only through compromise that we can govern under that Constitution. It is a lesson that seems to be completely lost thus far in 21st Century America.

Checks and Balances
Given the inherent shortcomings of humankind, effective government requires a balance of distributed power to check the potential excesses of each authority.

As the Constitutional delegates arrived in Philadelphia, a theoretical concept of "checks and balances" preexisted in no one's mind. What was on each person's mind was that a costly war had recently been fought in response to excesses in the rule of a central government; yet too weak a central government had proven ineffective in protecting the Union against external threats or generating the significant potential benefits from a merging of strengths. Balancing the freedoms of the people with the powers needed for government to be effective was tricky; balancing the need for action with the need to limit excessive powers *within* the government itself was equally tricky.

The concept of "checks and balances" was therefore a *creative response* to the difficulties the delegates encountered in reaching agreements given their many differing views on governmental power and its obligations:

- How much power should be given to the federal government, and how should it be distributed in such a way that no one arm of the government would have disproportionate authority?

- Should power be derived from the all-powerful states or should power be derived from the people?

- Should authority be vested in the primacy of the legislature (Congress) or a President?

- How much participation in government should be proper for the common man versus the educated and propertied elite?

- How should "majority rules" be balanced with protecting "minority rights" from oppression?

James Madison (VA) observed in the Federalist Papers that "What is government itself but the greatest of all reflections on human nature? If men were angels, no government would be necessary. If angels were to govern men, neither external nor internal controls on government would be necessary."[3] (It was a thought that could just as easily been written by Thomas Paine.) And Alexander Hamilton (NY) further stated that "If government is in the hands of a few, they will tyrannize the many; if in the hands of the many, they will tyrannize over the few."[4]   Thomas Jefferson (VA) expressed his concern that "All, too, will bear in mind this sacred principle, that though the will of the majority is in all cases to prevail, that will to be rightful must be reasonable; that the minority possess their equal rights, which equal law must protect and to violate would be oppression."[5]

But men and women are not angels; government is necessary; internal controls on government are necessary. So a proposed law requires each house of Congress to agree by majority vote; then the president must agree; if the president does not agree, s/he can veto it and prevent it; if Congress does not agree with the veto, they can override it by a 2/3rd vote; if the people do not like it, they can protest by having the Supreme Court review its constitutionality or adjudge its proper enforcement. No one facet of government is allowed to wreak its individual will unchecked. *All power is held in check, effectively balanced against the rights and authority of others, demanding of reasonable compromise as shown in the original Convention. This prescient planning is one of the most outstanding accomplishments of the Constitutional delegates toward governing a diverse society.* Even if they backed into it by accident.

Literal Interpretation of the Constitution
Words are a human invention, ambiguous at best, interpreted by each person's individual experience. The challenge for humans is how well each person brings his/her unique experiences to a common understanding.

Every election season we hear many contemporary politicians call for "strict constructionist" judges who will interpret the Constitution "literally" rather than inserting their own ideas for what they *think* it should mean. It all makes for good rhetorical headlines during an election campaign, and implies that one's devilish opponent is in favor of ignoring the Constitution or –

108

worse still – deliberately *mis*interpreting it. Yet how does one interpret a document literally when it was *intentionally designed to be non-literal*? As noted previously, Edmund Randolph (VA), primary drafter of the final wording of the Constitution and certainly no fan of "excess government," had established that in the writing of the Constitution itself to, a) "insert principle only..." and b) "use simple and precise language, and general propositions ..."[6] *A constitution is not a law; it is the basis for laws to be subsequently enacted.* A "law" must be very precise and stand on its own wording. A "constitution" reflects guiding principles which must be *translated* into specifics and details by subsequent laws and actions flowing from it. Also, like many biblical texts, a constitution often uses words from a point in time that have meaning unique to those times and circumstances; interpreting those words requires a knowledge of history and context as much as it does constitutional jurisprudence.

The words of the 2nd Amendment to the Constitution in our Bill of Rights state that: "A well regulated Militia, being necessary to the security of a free State, the right of the people to keep and bear Arms, shall not be infringed." It is all very specific; it is all very ambiguous. It says at the outset that any Militia should be *regulated*. In 1791 when this amendment was adopted, "arms" consisted only of pistol, musket and canon, all capable of only a single shot; are these the only arms to be protected? Conversely, does this 2nd Amendment "principle" preclude limiting *which* arms may be kept versus unlimited types of arms? Does it disallow limits on where these arms may be kept, or brought to, or what utilized for? The answers to these and other questions can be justifiably argued from many different points of view. In truth, there are very few "literals" in the provisions of the Constitution that an eight lane highway could not be driven through given the all too real shortcomings of the English language, the 200 year old timeframe in which it was written, and the stated intent that this Constitution would reflect *principles* of good government, not the

109

details. Our Constitution is intended to *guide* us, not to dictate to us.

Static Or Living Constitution
Creations can only be reflective of the view and moment in time in which they live. As with all things, to survive requires to adapt.

Related to the "literal" issue is another ambiguity regarding the supposed stability of our Constitution: is it to be a "static" document, anchored in a point in time and a particular set of circumstances? Or is it to be a "living" constitution, evolving with the times in order to be relevant and responsive to challenges impossible to foresee at the time of its creation?

Once again, our reference is the conservative, small-government proponent Edmund Randolph himself. His goal in writing the Constitution was to "insert principle only, lest the operations of government should be clogged by rendering those provisions permanent and unalterable, *which ought to be accommodated to times and events [emphasis added].*"[7] Thomas Jefferson, ever the foe of an overbearing central government, was emphatic on this point: "Some men look at Constitutions with sanctimonious reverence and deem them like the Arc of the Covenant – too sacred to be touched."[8]

Words, sentences and paragraphs create great confusion every day in our writings and conversations. Political demagogues can find support for their argument within the text of the Constitution regardless of whichever side of an issue they may be on. It is just as with preachers who can find biblical text to support either side of most moral arguments. We have to look at the issue at hand, and then understand the *overarching intention* of the Founders (versus the individual words) that the Founders sought to achieve around that issue. It is in that *intention* expressed by *Constitutional principles* where we will find our guidance.

110

"I am not an advocate for frequent changes in laws and constitutions, but laws and constitutions must go hand in hand with the progress of the human mind. As that becomes more developed, more enlightened, as new discoveries are made, new truths discovered and manners and opinions change, with the change of circumstances, institutions must advance also to keep pace with the times. We might as well require a man to wear still the coat which fitted him when a boy as civilized society to remain ever under the regimen of their barbarous ancestors."[9]

(Thomas Jefferson)

Extension of Democracy

*America and its government came from the **people**, by the **people**, for the benefit of the **people**. But the founders did not give participation in government to all of the people.*

In our popular mythology regarding America's founding, we believe that our Founders brought democracy to the common man by a recognition that "all men are created equal." Nothing could be further from the truth. The mechanisms that would *eventually* extend democracy and equality to all citizens of the country are contained in the Constitution. But it would take hundreds of years, changes in that Constitution, pursuing a work still in process, to fully bring equality and democracy to all of the people.

Most all of the founding fathers were highly suspicious, if not contemptuous, of the idea of all Americans participating fully in government. Only men, of education and with property were seen as qualified to lead the new government. The common man, without education and/or property, was not seen as qualified to understand the issues of the day, and was likely to attack wealth to

111

compensate for his lesser economic position. The Founders recognized that the common person was the ultimate source of government, and that government existed to protect and support their well-being. But they were also concerned about protecting their current station, and therefore a republican form of government was preferable to a fully democratic one. (Nevertheless, Thomas Jefferson observed that "I am not among those who fear the people. They, and not the rich, are our dependence for continued freedom."[10]) But the result was the institution of the selection of the President by a separately elected Electoral College; the election of senators by state legislatures; the appointment of Supreme Court judges by a President and confirmed by a Senate; and various state and federal voting restrictions that limited the right to vote. Only the House of Representatives was directly elected by the populace; but that is exactly why it was felt there needed to be checks on the power of that populace body.

More troubling were all of the other American residents who were restricted in their voting rights and legal status. Women, as was the custom in those days, had virtually no rights other than as attachments to (if not property of) their fathers or husbands. It is telling that the question of "female citizenship" was never even a topic of constitutional discussion, so deeply was this status quo embedded in American society. Changes in the constitutional status for women would not come about until the early 20th Century with the right to vote; many legal rights of property would not begin to come until the 1970s. Achievement of full economic and employment rights for women is still a work in process.

Slavery was the biggest hypocrisy of our founding. Even as the Declaration of Independence and then the Constitution were being voted upon, many delegates knew there was a failure in truth as to their achievements. The Declaration ignored the hypocrisy; the Constitution made a small dent by stopping the future import of slaves, but leaving current slaves intact. "All men are created equal," but in our constitutional beginnings not all men were allowed to exercise that freedom. It would take a costly (in dollars and lives) four-year war between most (but not all) of the slaveholding and the non-slaveholding states, and the 13th, 14th, and 15th amendments to the Constitution, to <u>officially</u> end slavery in America. But it took another 100 years thereafter to earnestly even begin to eliminate *de facto* slavery. It is still another work in process.

Millions of immigrants to this country in the ensuing years since the founding have had to work their way up through discrimination. Each group in their time – the Irish, the Asians, the Eastern Europeans, the Middle Easterners – have had to seemingly repeat their way through the original American colonial experience of survival, then education, then wealth before finally being fully welcomed into the American society. It is still another work in process.

So the Founders did not bring full citizenship and full rights immediately to all of society. They did not even design a democratic approach to government. For whatever larger reasons, history and civilization seem committed to such extensions being done on an incremental level. Likely each group needs its own time of preparation and experience in order to manage self-government, just as we see today that modern countries cannot adopt constitutional forms overnight without encountering major difficulties (e.g. Russia and Iraq). So the Magna Carta extended rights down from king to noblemen. The English Bill of Rights extended rights to Parliament – a *representative* of the English people. The American Founders extended most rights to the educated and propertied man, with the common man served through his elected representatives. Generations of Americans thereafter, by war or amendment or law or policy or judicial decree, are continually being extended those rights towards their natural objective – *that all people are free with certain unalienable rights*. With America as its laboratory, civilization is gradually getting to where it naturally and ultimately seeks to be.

"Justice is indiscriminately due to all, without regard to numbers, wealth, or rank."[11] So said John Jay, our first Chief Justice, writing for the Supreme Court in 1794. It is still a work in process.

Government Efficiency
Despots are highly efficient in telling people what to do. Listening to what diverse people need, where they want to go, and how to get there for the many is very messy and necessarily highly inefficient. But it is a required messiness for a free society.

Another popular political slogan, especially in poor economic times, is that "government ought to be run like a business." Implied is that government is wasteful, bureaucratic, and unable to respond quickly to needs. And so various candidates trot out before us proclaiming their success as businessmen/women, pointing fingers at "government insiders" as being inherently inadequate to run the government.

It is true that government is inherently not particularly efficient, though it ought to be expected to be responsive and to minimize any waste of resources supplied by the citizenry. But it is also true that government is NOT a business and therefore should not be run like one. Business has a particular product that it sells to a specific constituency who desires that product. It measures success by a definable measure – the dollars it profited. It operates by a "command and control" chain of authority, with decisions made by the highest rung (CEO) on the institutional pyramid and effected by legions of workers following orders. No matter how highly decentralized, delegated, consensus-based, or decision-by-committee structured the organization may claim to be, any such granting of authority downward is still at the organizational and

114

operational discretion of that CEO and his/her authorized subordinates.

America had that form of government once before. It was the English King, dictating decisions to his subjects (workers). America fought a revolution to reject that form of government. To be a bottom up government of We the People requires that the voices of the people be heard as to their desires and preferred directions, and then those many voices must be synthesized into a cohesive set of actions using a necessarily elaborate set of mechanisms. Those mechanisms must also ensure that extreme beliefs do not lurch the country down false pathways, hence the need for all of the checks and balances and expectations of compromise discussed above.

Not be wasteful? Be good stewards of resources appropriated from the citizens? Of course. Be efficient? God forbid, most certainly no. In George Washington's perspective, "Democratic States must always feel before they can see: it is this that makes their Governments slow, but the people will be right at last."[12] In government (versus business), getting it as close to right as possible, for the most people possible, is the more important goal.

Knowledge and Free Speech
Only an educated people can exercise freedom responsibly.

A critical factor in the success of the Revolution, and more so in the drafting and ratification of the Constitution, was the recognition by our Founders in the value, if not absolute necessity, of the guarantee and promotion of free speech and a free press to disseminate that speech. Guttenberg had provided the mechanical means through his movable type printing press. Benjamin Franklin achieved his earliest successes as a printer working with the descendant machinery of that press. Philosophers, historians and lawyers informed the thinking of our founding, and writers and pamphleteers and newspaper editors spread their perspectives and proposals across the fledging nation to influence "public opinion." But such informing required an educated reader able to receive and process those ideas and discriminate among conflicting opinions. Without an educated citizen, able to write his/her ideas and disseminate them widely to a similarly educated audience capable of receiving and critically assessing them, the creation of America simply would not have been possible. In a democracy, education and an informed public were seen as crucial to the long-term survival of the Republic.

Even in its early infancy, the country had already taken steps to promote education – even if initially for the wealthier class who could afford this "luxury." Generally, learning occurred in private study (typically from ministers), by mentoring from men already in the existing professions, by women in the home, or by self-study. (Public education in the schoolhouse for the masses would have to wait until the mid-1800s.) But wealthier colonists began early on to create places for the higher education for their children. Harvard, the first college, was founded as early as 1636, only 16 years after the Pilgrims landed. The College of William and Mary followed in 1693; Yale in 1701; Academy of Philadelphia (now University of Pennsylvania) in 1740; College of New Jersey (now Princeton University) in 1746; King's College (now Columbia University) in 1754; Rhode Island College (now Brown University) in 1764; Queen's College (now Rutgers University) in 1766; and Dartmouth College in 1769. These colleges gave the colonies a north-to-south access to higher learning early on in America's development. Regardless of how each had achieved their education, the Founders were fierce in their support of learning and information for the future sake of the country. They knew the impact that the written words of Thomas Paine and other writers had had on the Revolutionary cause and making the case for the new Constitution. And so they guaranteed the right to free speech and a free press in the very first Amendment of the Bill of Rights. ("Let us dare to read, think, speak and write."[13] John

Adams) So let us appropriately hear directly from some of the Founders about the importance of education, free speech and free press:

On Education and Knowledge:
Thomas Jefferson: "I have sworn upon the altar of God eternal hostility against every form of tyranny over the mind of man."[14]

James Madison: "A popular government without popular information, or the means of acquiring it, is but a prologue to a farce or a tragedy; or, perhaps both. Knowledge will forever govern ignorance. And a people who mean to be their own governors must arm themselves with the power which knowledge gives."[15]

Thomas Jefferson: "I know of no safe depository of the ultimate powers of society but the people themselves; and if we think them not enlightened enough to exercise their control with a wholesome discretion, the remedy is not to take it from them, but to inform their discretion by education."[16]

John Adams: "Liberty cannot be preserved without a general knowledge among the people, who have a right … and a desire to know; but besides this, they have a right, an undisputable, unalienable, indefeasible, divine right to that most dreaded and envied kind of knowledge, I mean of the characters and conduct of their rulers."[17]

Thomas Jefferson: "The most important bill in our whole code is that for the diffusion of knowledge among the people. No other sure foundation can be devised, for the preservation of freedom and happiness."[18]

On Freedom of Speech:
Benjamin Franklin: "In those wretched countries where a man cannot call his tongue his own, he can scarcely call anything his

own. Whoever would overthrow the liberty of a nation must begin by subduing the freeness of speech; a terrible thing to publick traytors."[19]

On Freedom of the Press:
Thomas Jefferson: "Our liberty depends on the freedom of the press, and that cannot be limited without being lost."[20]

Alexander Hamilton" "The liberty of the press consists in the right to publish with impunity truth with good motives, for justifiable ends. To disallow it is fatal."[21]

Thomas Jefferson: "I am for ... freedom of the press and against all violations of the Constitution to silence by force, and not by reason, the complaints or criticisms, just or unjust, of our citizens against the conduct of their agents."[22]

Thomas Jefferson: "To the press alone, chequered as it is with abuses, the world is indebted for all the triumphs which have been gained by reason and humanity over error and oppression."[23]

As bitter enemies as they subsequently proved to be over their differences in the role of government, and as much as each was personally attacked in the press, Jefferson, Hamilton and others were nevertheless together in their views on the necessity of widespread education, free speech, and a free press – however personally discomforting it might be.

Divine Intervention?
To whatever form and impetus we may ascribe as being its source, America was not just a purely human accomplishment at one isolated moment in time.

Was America's founding an act of Divine Intervention, the March of History, inspired human beings, or just dumb luck?   It

118

ultimately comes down to what you choose to believe. But in looking at the historical threads recounted in this narrative, it would be very difficult to say that America was merely a random accident of just human events and their meandering doings.

Certainly most all of the founders believed that what they were doing was ascribed to a much larger purpose than just the immediacy of their own needs for their own selves. They offered perspectives such as:

- "It is a common observation here (in Paris) that our cause is the cause of all mankind, and that we are fighting for their liberty in defending our own."[24] (Benjamin Franklin, echoing Thomas Paine's writings)

- "I always consider the settlement of America with reverence and wonder, as the opening of a grand scene and design in Providence for the illumination of the ignorant, and the emancipation of the slavish part of mankind over all the earth."[25] (John Adams)

- "The God who gave us life, gave us liberty at the same time."[26] (Thomas Jefferson, in a remark said before writing the Declaration of Independence)

- "Kings or Parliaments could not give the rights essential to happiness … we claim them from a higher source – from the King of Kings, and the Lord of all the Earth. They are not annexed to us by parchments or seals. They are created in us by the decrees of Providence which established the laws of our nature. They are born with us; exist with us; and cannot be taken from us by any human power without taking our lives."[27] (John Dickinson)

- "The citizens of America … are, from this period, to be considered as the actors on a most conspicuous theater, which seems to be peculiarly designated by Providence for

119

the display of human greatness and felicity."[28]   (George Washington)

The Revolutionary leaders and the Constitutional delegates frequently intoned privately their individual hopes that God (Providence) would shine on them and guide their work. Near the end of the Constitutional Convention, Benjamin Franklin (PA) would observe, "I have lived, sir, a long time, and the longer I live, the more convincing proofs I see of this truth – that God Governs in the affairs of men. And if a sparrow cannot fall to the ground without His notice, is it probable that an empire can rise without His aid?"[29] Months after the Convention's close, Madison would state that "it is impossible for the man of pious reflection not to perceive in [the Constitution] a finger of the Almighty hand which has been so frequently and signally extended to our relief in the critical stages of the revolution."[30] Benjamin Rush (PA) went even further and said that "the hand of God was employed in this work, as that God divided the Red Sea to give a passage to the children of Israel."[31] And George Washington stated in his first Inaugural Address, "No people can be bound to acknowledge and adore the invisible hand, which conducts the Affairs of men more than the People of the United States. Every step, by which they have advanced to the character of an independent nation, seems to have been distinguished by some token of providential agency."[32]

Yet while many of the Founders may have felt they may have been instruments in God's hand and fulfilling God's expectations of them, they nevertheless were highly cautious about ever using that as a defense of their work, or an argument for ratification, or a desire to incorporate any such divine language into their output. When Benjamin Franklin (PA) proposed beginning each session of the Constitutional Convention with prayer for "… the Father of lights to illuminate our understandings,"[33] his proposal went nowhere and no such prayer routine was ever adopted. Franklin quietly noted that "The convention, except three or four persons, thought prayers unnecessary."[34] Such reluctance by the delegates

120

likely reflected their overall cautious attitudes regarding the intermixing of religious and governmental institutions or involvements.

XIII. RELIGION AND THE FOUNDING OF AMERICA

Religion in America, and its place in the minds of the Founders and within the body and spirit of the Constitution, deserves some special commentary. Throughout our history as a Republic, but more recently during the last decade of the 20th Century and the first decade of the 21st Century, there has been a sustained drive by some citizens to merge religion and government into an interdependent relationship. There have been calls for government funding of activities that are clearly religious-based in nature, however commendable might be their intention. There have been attempts to overthrow judicial rulings that have prevented the religious speech of one individual religion from being advocated in public forums that contain citizens of multiple religions in attendance. There have been attempts to legally maximize one religion's dogma, ethics or observances to the diminution of other religions.

More recently, there has been an argument advocated in some quarters that America was founded as, and is, "a Christian Nation." Although it is not clear towards what ends such advocates are attempting this troublesome labeling (other than it being a justifying call towards their own presumed righteousness), one assumes that religious favoritism in legislation and governmental actions is the ultimately intended purpose. Most troubling in this advocacy is that the justification for America's being "a Christian Nation" is not a proposal for the future for which there would be a fresh national debate. Rather, it is an argument pointed backwards, an attempt to close the debate before it starts, premised on the belief that the Founders themselves intended for America to be a Christian nation from the beginning.

Such a claim of a Christian Nation could not be a bigger distortion of the Founders' true intentions for America, or even many of the early colonists. Even where religious differences were not tolerated *within* a community (e.g. in Puritan communities) and resulted in banishment, people generally lived in mutual toleration of their differences from one community to another. People just mutually agreed to leave each community to its own practice as long as they themselves were left alone. The freedom to practice one's own faith undisturbed was held to be a fundamental right from living in America, indeed for coming to America at all. Absolute freedom of religious practice is in fact one of the few instances where near unanimity of thought can be found in the thinking of the Revolutionary and Constitutional Founders.

The claim that America was founded as a Christian Nation is distorted thinking, a misrepresentation debunked based upon five considerations:
- Christianity and the European Heritage
- The Religious Diversity of Colonial America
- The Differing Views of the Founders' Religious Thoughts
- The Separation of Church and State
- The Words of the Founders Themselves

Let us examine each of these five considerations both singularly and in combination.

Christianity and the European Heritage
It is certainly true that most of the settlers to English America were of the Christian faith. But that is less a statement about America's intention and more a truth reflecting the backgrounds of these immigrants. As we saw in previous chapters, by the 1600s Europe had become a collection of many nations, each distinctive and different in character and outlook. Religion had broken up from one comprehensive Catholic Church into many smaller religious

affiliations reflecting widely different perspectives about God and Christianity. These breakups would continue to expand throughout the 1600s and 1700s, often incurring great persecution and generating much conflict. Many of these persecuted people needed a new place where they could practice their religion freely and openly. And an empty America needed people to populate it if it was going to fulfill part of its Purpose – *to show what people are capable of when working together among diverse opinions and backgrounds.* So the people it needed were these Europeans – specifically <u>because</u> they were richly diverse, tired of the old European story of continual conflict and repression, and unable to get along with each other up to this point.

Europe contained diversity in many forms: culture, language, learning, religion, trade skills, political thought, social traditions, nationalities. This diversity was exactly what was needed in America as the raw material for its experiment in "unified diversity." People's religious affiliations provided a significant diversity around a highly personal subject which expressed their individuality and desire for freedom. Yet the common experience of their Christianity gave them a sufficiently shared link to hold them together and not let their diversity drive them too far apart. Christianity provided the perfect balance needed.

(Non-Christian immigration – e.g. Islam, Buddhism – would therefore hold off until later in the 20th Century; Islam and Buddhism were already doing valuable work in other parts of the globe, and their presence in 1600s America would have stretched the early colonists' capacities for tolerance too far for that moment in time. Non-Christian Native-Americans and African-American slaves were already being ignored or marginalized by white European colonists as being <u>too</u> inferior and different.)

The unfortunate truth about Christianity is that it has rarely been a unifying force among people, quite in contrast to the great unifying messages offered by Jesus. After the first Century CE, Christianity is a history filled with all-too-human conflict, persecution within the Christian Church against those of differing practice or dogma, and political schemes for individual or organizational domination. All of which undermined the many great positive contributions also provided by the Church. For many parishioners or religious leaders, either at the organizational level or within local churches, Christianity has been a never-ending argument about who is the "true Christian," rather than embracing and accepting the many forms that legitimate belief and worship can take. "Who's right" has all too often been the priority, with each denomination typically defined more by its differences than its commonality within its founder Jesus. So one nation – America – could not possibly be one religion – Christianity – because whose version of Christianity would you then define America to be? And which versions of Christianity would be willing to surrender themselves to the one selected? In the end, if one argues for one Christian nation, then you have to accept that there is only one Christian religion. And that would simply defy the whole story of American colonization and independence, as well as the history of Christianity itself.

The Religious Diversity of Colonial America

It is true that all of the signers of the Constitution were members of some branch of the Christian religion. Yet the religious affiliations of the Constitutional delegates, and their commitment to religious observance, ritual and church attendance, differed extensively from delegate to delegate. Their religious affiliation was primarily a reflection of the religion prevalent in each person's geographical residence as well as their personal and professional affiliations. While a specific geographic location could often be defined by one predominant religion, across the thirteen states those religions varied given the backgrounds of the colonists and their motivations for immigration. Certainly the major forms of religion were found across the young nation, mainly Episcopal (Anglican), Congregational, Presbyterian and Baptist. Given that America was so recently separated from England's control, where the Anglican Church was the official religion of the Church of England, it is no surprise that in 1790 the majority of the American population was affiliated with the Anglican Church reflecting their deep cultural, social and commercial ties with England. Following the Revolutionary War and America's separation from England, in 1789 American Anglicans established the independent Episcopal Church, separating from the Anglican Church and rejecting religious superiority and loyalty to the King. As the country then grew and other Protestant religions took root in America, the relative size of the Episcopal Church diminished to most recently being the 14th largest denomination in America.

In addition to these predominant religions, smaller numbers of Anabaptist (under various forms and names) and Lutherans populated the country, and Methodists were just getting started in America near the end of the 1700s. Certain religions were highly concentrated in particular areas: Quakers in Pennsylvania, Delaware and Rhode Island; Dutch Reformed in New York and New Jersey; Catholics in Maryland; Jews in the several major port cities of the nation.

But alongside these familiar names were also smaller religious sects dotted throughout the landscape. Many of these sects were based upon differing views of simplicity of worship and/or religious organizational structure, or questioning beliefs regarding the Christian Trinity, or a kinship to the beliefs or practices of the earliest Christians in the first century after Jesus' death. They were often found in the backcountry, with an embedded tradition of enjoying full religious rights, respect, and freedom of practice from their neighbors. Their churches (if any) were often side-by-side with the mainline churches, and they enjoyed good relations with their neighbors of other beliefs. These included groups such as the:

- Shakers, Universalists and Unitarians in New England;

- Moravians in Pennsylvania, North Carolina and Georgia;

- Mennonites and Schwenkfelders in Pennsylvania;

- The Brethren in western Pennsylvania, Virginia and Maryland;

- The Ephrata Community of Lancaster, Pennsylvania (an offspring of the Brethren).

This religious diversity was much in evidence in the Constitutional Convention itself. Among the delegates, there were 31 Episcopalians (over half of the participants), 16 Presbyterians, 8 Congregationalists, 3 Quakers, 2 Catholics, 2 Methodists, 2 Lutherans, and 2 Dutch Reformed.[1] In addition to this diversity of religions, Massachusetts, Rhode Island, Pennsylvania, and Maryland had been founded to some degree driven by a quest for freedom of religious practice – even if that freedom was not always extended to persons of other faiths (e.g. Massachusetts). Clearly a tradition of religious affiliation, but with freedom, tolerance and diversity, has been a deep part of the American fabric from early on.

The Differing Views of the Founders' Religious Thoughts
The late $17^{th} \rightarrow 18^{th}$ Century was yet another new period of intellectual growth. It was the "Age of Reason" (or Age of Enlightenment) that saw a flourishing of new thinking in philosophy, science, and the "rights of man" – all driven by an emphasis on logical, rational thought. The movement was centered in France, drew in thinkers from all over Europe, and included familiar names such as Voltaire, John Locke, Baruch Spinoza, and Issac Newton, all fed by our familiar friend – the printing press. Such an emphasis on pure logic and reasoning led to the growth of Deism in religious thinking. These Deists believed that: a) applying reasoning to a keen observation of the natural world will lead to a conclusion that the World and the

Universe beyond are products of a Creator God; b) once the world was created, it runs on its own according to the natural laws and mechanisms created by that God; and c) therefore such a God is absent from the daily conduct of human affairs (a non-interventionist God). Applying these premises to religious thinking, Deists concluded that a) God has no need to be revealed through miracles or displays in human form; b) the writings of the Christian Bible were subject to human error; and c) God existed, but in one and only one form, hence the idea of the Trinity (God as Father and Son and Holy Spirit) was in error. It also led to considering God as a less personal, knowable figure, hence the predominant use of "Spirit" or "Providence" or other descriptive but neutral language references to this Divine Creator.

This Enlightenment and Deist thinking made its way to America and found many adherents among the Founders. While all of the Founders were believers in God (some more passionately than others), Deist thinking led to a variety of individual belief systems on the subject of God, Jesus and religion regardless of one's formal religious affiliation. Some shared the Deist thinking of a removed God; others retained a belief in some level of an interventionist God, while still adopting much other Deist thinking against miracles or the Trinity. (This anti-Trinity stance was also another form of anti-Catholicism, which many Anglicans were.) Let us look at four examples of such differing beliefs.

Thomas Paine's writing (including his treatises "Rights Of Man" and "The Age of Reason" in the 1790s) reflected a strong belief in Deist thinking and human rights. Paine was often accused of being an atheist due to his attacks on religion, but his writings reflected a strong belief in God and a belief that it was the Christian Church itself that had abandoned the teachings of God and Jesus. He wrote in the Age of Reason that "I believe in one God, and no more; and I hope for happiness beyond this life. I believe in the equality of man and I believe that religious duties consist of doing justice, loving mercy, and endeavoring to make our fellow-creatures happy."[2]

Benjamin Franklin wrote in his Autobiography "for the arguments of the Deists ... appeared to me much stronger than the refutations; in short, I soon became a thorough Deist."[3]   Nevertheless, he qualified this later by saying that "the Deity sometimes interferes by his particular Providence, and sets aside the Events which would have otherwise been produc'd in the Course of Nature, or by the Free Agency of Man."[4]   It became a semi-interventionist stance.

George Washington, circumspect in his religious views as with most all things, is harder to characterize religiously. He was a member of the Episcopal Church (common for Virginians of his day), but an infrequent churchgoer. He clearly believed in God, but in his public correspondence he used the Deist language of "Providence," the "Deity," "the Grand Architect," etc. He made minimal use of the term "God," and made virtually no reference to Jesus. By the accounts of his contemporaries, he never received communion from the Episcopal Church (normally a required sacrament of worshipers), and asked for no priest at his bedside death.   (The story is told that, when attending services at an Episcopal Church in Philadelphia, the priest spoke out against "... those in elevated stations who invariably turned their backs upon the celebration of the Lord's Supper [communion]."[5]   While the priest likely may have expected his admonition to cause a change in people's conduct and Washington to set a better example, instead Washington said nothing and simply never returned to that church again!)   Like many Deists, he put his emphasis on promoting strict ethics of conduct, and took life's circumstances as they came.   In describing Washington's religious views, James Madison said that he "does not suppose that Washington ever attended to the arguments for Christianity, and for the differing systems of religion, or in fact that he had formed definite opinions on the subject."[6] Washington saw to his own morality and ethics, and strongly encouraged others to do the same. But he appears to have left dogma to the debates of others.

John Adams was raised in the Congregationalist Church, but adopted many Deist views as a young adult. He believed fully in God and in Jesus as the Son of God, but came to reject the idea of the Trinity and the divinity of Jesus. He was a devout supporter of Christianity, but more skeptical of established Christian religion. He observed that "This would be the best of all possible Worlds, if there were no religion in it," yet went on to qualify that "without Religion this World would be Something not fit to be mentioned in polite company, I mean Hell."[7] His apparent goal was a middle way – enlightened Christianity: "Let the human mind loose. It must be loosed; it will be loosed. Superstition and despotism cannot confine it."[8]

It is also worth noting that George Washington, and perhaps as many as one-third of the Constitutional signers, were members of the Freemasons, a religious fraternal organization. Freemasons require a belief in God for membership, but leave the interpretation of God to one's own belief. Thus all forms of belief in God are acceptable – including non-Christian / non-Trinitarian ones. This obligation of religious freedom has to be assumed to have also guided the Founders thinking about religious freedom and practice in America.

Like many simple questions that have no simple answers, one can accurately say that the Founders were of the Christian faith. But presuming that they were therefore of common mind on the subject of God, Jesus or religion in general, or that being "Christian" meant the same thing to each of them, or the same as what it means to be a Christian in the 21st Century, would belie the truth of their convictions.

The Separation of Church and State

So did the Founders intend for America to be a Christian nation, or any other version of a "religious nation?" Certainly at the time of the writing of the Constitution, examples of the intermixing of "church and state" existed. The Puritans favored merging church and state: since all things are within and expressions of God, all must be "purified." This included government which was responsible for maintaining the order of the colony. (A similar position would be promoted by groups such as the Shakers – no division between the spiritual and secular worlds.) Eight of the colonies formally designated a particular "state religion," either Anglican or Congregational; Delaware, Rhode Island, Georgia, Pennsylvania and New Jersey specified none. Such designation of a particular state religion usually affected tax benefits accruing to the Church, limitations on eligibility to vote or hold public office based upon one's religion, or mandating church attendance.

Virginia, New York and Delaware each developed some legal statement regarding religious freedom. Yet in all 13 of the states the degree of religious tolerance at one time or another had various limitations on whether religious rights extended only to Christians. As the country moved out of its Constitutional infancy, and with the standard of religious freedom set at the federal level in the First Amendment, support for any designated religion died away in the states. Either through constitutional amendment or revised constitutions, any religious preferences or restrictions were eliminated in most all states by the mid-1800s. Any restrictions then remaining were invalidated by the 14th Amendment passed after the Civil War which provided for: an expanded eligibility of citizenship; due process of the law by each state to be applied equally to all citizens; and the provision of equal protection to each citizen.

So does this background of state and religion intermixing, or restricting religious rights only to one given group (i.e. Christians), argue for America being a Christian nation? No, because such a mix only worked for a limited period of time and only at a local level. As noted before, immigration was all European, and Europe was almost entirely state-sponsored Christian, so Christianity was the known shared cultural background. Up until the late 1700s, the American colonies lived remotely and highly separately from each other. States were the primary power; populations were relatively homogeneous at the state or local level. When the thirteen individual states sought to come together as one independent nation, the Revolutionary War and the forming of a national government necessitated that Americans have more substantial interaction among themselves. From that greater interaction they had to acknowledge the significant differences that existed among them socially and religiously, and thereby the potential threat to their continued individual expression of faith and monopoly on religion. Localism had to give way to nationalism.

Times were changing – in the political and legal environment, in the movements of the population into more heterogeneous settings, and in the continuing breakup of Christian unity into more and more separate denominations and sects. Religious and political leaders with greater foresight realized that the favored religion of today could just as easily become the sideline religion of tomorrow. Who is to say what religion will become the favored one, given the mistrust of each Christian denomination towards the others? Most religious leaders want to be left alone to follow their practice. Yet once government starts to be your "partner," there will always rightfully be some form of quid pro quo expected in return (i.e. government starts to interfere). For enlightened clergy, partnering with the state is not worth the risk of having the state tell the preacher what to do and not do. History is the proof.

Politically, the many Deists among the political leaders were already highly skeptical of the established religions and the role of the clergy in state affairs. The Founders knew world history all too well, and they knew the outcomes and historical experiences of blending church and state in the Roman Empire and in Europe, and the incessant conflicts that that had engendered, and the diminution of moral authority that resulted. Individual freedom was the point of the Revolution; resistance to big government was standard thinking. For the Founders, a church intertwined with the state does not lead to freedom. So in the Constitution and the early Bill of Rights, their decision was that there would be no affirmative mention of either God or religion; such a decision otherwise could have proven just as divisive as the representation or slavery issue. It was troublesome territory not worth marching into. In fact the only two explicit mentions of religion made were in the negative:

- "No religious Test shall ever be required as a Qualification to any office or public Trust under the United States." (Article VI, U.S. Constitution, originally proposed by delegate Charles Pinckney [SC]. Note the sweeping broadness and absoluteness of the statement, made without qualification, without any "except for ...")

- "Congress shall make no law respecting an establishment of religion, or prohibiting the free exercise thereof ..." (The very first words in the very First Amendment – the First Right – adopted to the Constitution within the Bill of Rights. It was deemed that important. Once again, note the sweeping broadness and absoluteness of the statement, made without qualification, without any "except for ...")

Today many religious and political leaders and news commentators decry instances of church/state governments that operate under a specific religious law – i.e. theocracies. Unfortunately, many of these objections are purely code words for masking discriminatory objections specifically to Islam and Islamic states in the greater Middle East area. However, such church/state intermixing is utilized in Israel (our strong ally). Formal state religions are still commonplace throughout the world reflecting a continuation of their long-term history: Lutheran in Denmark, Finland, Iceland, Sweden and Norway; Catholic in Monaco, Malta, Costa Rica, some parts of Switzerland, and with "special recognition" status in

133

Italy, Poland, Spain, the Philippines and South America; and, of course, Anglican in England.

The fact that America's Founders were all affiliated with some form of Christian denomination by dint of birth and upbringing does not demand that the output of their creative work be a religiously-designated nation. "Being" is not the same as "intending." Henry Ford was a life-long Episcopalian. It is very likely that his Episcopalian upbringing had certain influences on his business decisions. However, we do not presume by his church membership that Mr. Ford intended to make only "Episcopalian cars" exclusively for Episcopalian buyers. Quite the contrary. Ford cars are available to anyone of any stripe; Ford cars are judged on the merits of their construction and quality, not on the religion of the company's founder. Given the history of America to 1790, would our Founders really want the exclusivity of any one religion for a nation as diverse as, and with the Purpose of, America?

When we read early colonist writings that reinforce "only Christianity," we need to remember the reality of Colonial America. There were a smattering of Jews throughout the colonies, along with "heretic" native religions. Otherwise, by dint of our European origination, *Christianity was the only religion known in Colonial America, and given its many divisions, it was the only known religion needing toleration among its parts.* Non-Christian religions would simply not become a significant presence in America until the 20th century, and these would rightfully expect to receive the full extension of religious freedom guaranteed to them – without limitation, without prejudice.

Perhaps our guidance should best come from the original Christian himself: "Render unto Caesar the things which are Caesar's, and unto God the things that are God's." (Matthew 22:21) It is the best advice from the best Advisor: keep church and state affairs and

134

involvements separate, and do right by each. Bound together, each will wind up corrupting the other.

The Words of the Founders Themselves

In the end, perhaps the most effective understanding of the intentions of the Founders regarding religion in America should come from them. So let us listen to some diverse representatives regarding their own thoughts on the subject:

"When I signed the Declaration of Independence I had in view not only our independence from England but the toleration of all sects."[9] (Charles Carroll, Maryland, Catholic, signer of the Declaration of Independence.)

"Driven from every corner of the earth, Freedom of Thought and The Right of Private Judgment in matters of conscience direct their course to this happy country as their last asylum."[10] (Samuel Adams, Massachusetts, Congregationalist, signer of the Declaration of Independence, in a speech at State House in Philadelphia, August, 1776.)

"Happy it is when the interest which the government has in the preservation of its own power, coincides with a proper distribution of the public burdens, and tends to guard the least wealthy part of the community from oppression!"[11] (Alexander Hamilton, New York, Huguenot/Presbyterian, signer of the Constitution.)

"No point is so plain, as that Morality is our Duty; for all Sides agree in that. A virtuous Heretick shall be saved before a wicked Christian."[12] (Benjamin Franklin, Pennsylvania, Episcopalian/Deist, signer of Declaration of Independence and Constitution.)

"The liberty enjoyed by the people of these States of worshiping Almighty God, agreeably to their consciences, is not only among

135

the choicest of their *blessings*, but also of their *rights*."[13] (George Washington, Virginia, Episcopalian, 1st President, writing to Quakers in 1789.)

"As mankind becomes more liberal, they will be more able to allow that those who conduct themselves as worthy members of the community are equally entitled to the protection of civil government. I hope ever to see America among the foremost nations in examples of justice and liberality."[14] (George Washington, writing to Catholics in 1789.)

"Government has no Right to hurt a hair of the head of an Atheist for his Opinions. Let him have a care of his Practices."[15] (John Adams, Massachusetts, Congregationalist/Unitarian, Signer of Declaration of Independence and 2nd president, in a letter to his son.)

"I will not condescend to employ the word Toleration. I assert that unlimited freedom of religion, consistent with morals and property, is essential to the progress of society and the amelioration of the condition of mankind."[16] (John Adams.)

Thomas Jefferson's Views (Virginia, Episcopalian/Deist):
Thomas Jefferson was one of the most important figures among the Founders. He was the principal author of the Declaration of Independence; drafter of the Virginia Statute for Religious Freedom; founder of the University of Virginia; the first Secretary of State; Vice President under John Adams; and third President of the United States. He remained as fierce an advocate of individual freedom, belief in the common man, and limited government as any of the Founders. He believed in God and in the purity of Jesus' teachings (though not Jesus' divinity), but had little enthusiasm for organized religion or the clergy given his observations of the negative results from state-sponsored religions. He created what is now known as "The Jefferson Bible" (originally

entitled "The Life and Morals of Jesus of Nazareth"), an extract of Jesus' words, excluding the miracle and divinity stories, in order to just focus on the absolute quality of those original teachings.

And so Mr. Jefferson might be the best to speak to us of the broad view of the issue of faith, government, skepticism of the clergy, and freedom of worship prevalent among many of the Founders:

"We are not in a world ungoverned by the laws and power of a superior agent. Our efforts are in his hand and directed by it; and he will give them their effect in his own time."[17]

"The doctrines of Jesus are simple, and tend all to the happiness of man. 1. That there is only one God, and he is all perfect. 2. That there is a future state of rewards and punishments. 3. That to love God with all thy heart and thy neighbor as thyself, is the sum of religion."[18]

"Had the doctrines of Jesus been preached always as purely as they came from his lips, the whole civilised world would now have been Christian."[19]

"I consider the doctrines of Jesus as delivered by himself to contain the outlines of the most sublime system of morality that has ever been taught but I hold in the most profound detestation and execration the corruptions of it which have been invented ..."[20]

"My opinion is that there would never have been an infidel, if there had never been a priest. The artificial structures they have built on the purest of all moral systems, for the purpose of deriving from it pence and power, revolts those who think for themselves, and who read in that system only what is really there."[21]

"It does me no injury for my neighbor to say there are twenty Gods, or no God."[22]

137

"Almighty God hath created the mind free. All attempts to influence it by temporal punishments or burdens … are a departure from the plan of the Holy Author of our religion … No man shall be compelled to frequent or support any religious worship or ministry or shall otherwise suffer on account of his religious opinions or belief, but all men shall be free to profess and by argument to maintain, their opinions in matters of religion. I know but one code of morality for men whether acting singly or collectively."[23]

"I have ever thought religion a concern purely between our God and our consciences, for which we were accountable to him, and not to the priests. I never told my own religion, nor scrutinized that of another. I never attempted to make a convert, nor wished to change another's creed. I have ever judged of the religion of others by their lives … For it is in our lives, and not from our words, that our religion must be read."[24]

Perhaps the final word on this subject should be a retrospective one. Robert E. Lee was born into one of the great Virginia founding families at the dawn of the 19th century, just as America was beginning the necessary work to fulfill the promise of its Founding. He was, and remains, the quintessential Southerner, marked by exemplary character, ethics, dedication to responsibility, and religious faith, revered by contemporary and descendant Southerners. Yet he observed, with great clarity:

> "Is it not strange that the descendants of those
> Pilgrim fathers who Crossed the Atlantic to
> preserve their own freedom of opinion had always
> proved themselves intolerant of the Spiritual liberty
> of others?"[25]

XIV. FINAL WORDS
FROM OUR FOUNDING FATHERS

"I have often ... in the course of the session ...
looked at that sun behind the President
without being able to tell whether it was rising or setting.
But now at length I have the happiness to know
it is a rising and not a setting sun."[1]

(Benjamin Franklin, on the last day of the Constitutional
Convention,
commenting on the carving in the back of George Washington's
chair.)

"America, an immense territory, favour'd by
nature with all advantages of climate, soil, great
navigable rivers and lakes, etc., was destined to
become a great country, populous and mighty;
and would in a less time than was generally
conceive'd be able to shake off any shackles
that might be impos'd on her, and perhaps place
them on the imposters."[2]

(Benjamin Franklin
from his Autobiography)

"They accomplished a revolution which has no
parallel in the annals of human society. They
reared the fabrics of governments which have
no model on the face of the globe. They formed

the design of a great Confederacy, which is incumbent on their successors to improve and perpetuate."[3]

(James Madison)

"The first month [of the Convention] we only came to grips, and the second it seemed as though we would fly apart forever, however we came as close as friends of eighty years in but days."[4]

(Daniel of Saint Thomas Jenifer
Constitutional delegate from Maryland)

"I like the dreams of the future better than the history of the past."[5]

(Thomas Jefferson)

Benjamin Franklin had said that the Founders had given us "A Republic, if you can keep it." Keeping that Republic necessarily requires that we follow in the footsteps of what those founders wrought. Not just their words. Not just their forms. But also in the Character, the Approach, and the Spirit within which they achieved what they did.

Keeping the Republic requires our time, our full efforts, and our constant diligence. Because those who would undermine this gift, appropriate it to their own selfish ends, and betray America's Purpose, are ever among us.

140

"Citizens, by birth or choice, of a common country, that country has a right to concentrate your affections. The name of American, which belongs to you in your national capacity, must always exalt the just pride of patriotism more than any appellation derived from local discriminations ..."[6]

"Guard against the impostures of pretended patriotism."[7]

(George Washington
from his Farewell Address upon his
retirement from a lifetime of Public Service)

The challenge is still before us.

APPENDIX 1:

THE FOUNDING FATHERS

The following identifies the **118** signers of the principal documents that founded the United States of America from 1776-1787; their state; their age at the time of their participation in the creation of the Declaration of Independence (Dec), and/or the Articles of Confederation (Conf), and/or the Constitution (Const).

1. **THE SIGNERS – AMERICA'S FOUNDING DOCUMENTS**:

NAME		1776 Dec	1781 Conf	1787 Const
Andrew Adams	CT		55	
John Adams	MA	40		
Samuel Adams	MA	53	58	
Thomas Adams	VA		51	
Abraham Baldwin	GA			33
John Banister	VA		47	
Josiah Bartlett	NH	46	51	
Richard Bassett	DE			42
Gunning Bedford, Jr.	DE			40
John Blair	VA			55
William Blount	NC			38
Pierce Butler	SC			43
Carter Braxton	VA	39		
David Brearley	NJ			42
Jacob Broom	DE			35
Charles Carroll	MD	38		
Daniel Carroll	MD		51	57
Samuel Chase	MD	35		

NAME		1776 Dec	1781 Conf	1787 Const
Abraham Clark	NJ	50		
William Clingan	PA		60	
George Clymer	PA	37		48
John Collins	RI		64[2]	
Francis Dana	MA		38	
Jonathan Dayton	NJ			27[1]
John Dickinson	DE		49	55
William H. Drayton	SC		39	
James Duane	NY		48	
William Duer	NY		38	
William Ellery	RI	48	53	
William Few, Jr.	GA			39
Thomas Fitzsimons	PA			46
William Floyd	NY	41		
Benjamin Franklin	PA	70[2]		81[2]
Elbridge Gerry	MA	32	37	X[4]
Nicholas Gilman	NH			32
Nathaniel Gorham	MA			49
Button Gwinnett	GA	41		
Lyman Hall	GA	52		
Alexander Hamilton	NY			32
John Hancock	MA	39	44	
John Hanson	MD		60	
Cornelius Harnett	NC		58	
Benjamin Harrison	VA	50		
John Hart	NJ	65		
John Harvie	VA		39	
Joseph Hewes	NC	46		
Thomas Heyward, Jr.	SC	30	35	
Samuel Holton	MA		43	
William Hooper	NC	34		
Stephen Hopkins	RI	69		

144

NAME		1776 Dec	1781 Conf	1787 Const
Francis Hopkinson	NJ	38		
Titus Hosmer	CT		55	
Samuel Huntington	CT	45	50	
Richard Hutson	SC		34	
Jared Ingersoll	PA			38
Thomas Jefferson	VA	33		
Daniel of St. T. Jenifer	MD			64
William S. Johnson	CT			60
Rufus King	MA			32
John Langdon	NH			46
Edward Langworthy	GA		43	
Henry Laurens	SC		37	
Richard Henry Lee	VA	44	49	
Francis Lightfoot Lee	VA	41	46	
Francis Lewis	NY	63	68	
Philip Livingston	NY	60		
William Livingston	NJ			64
James Lovell	MA		44	
Thomas Lynch, Jr.	SC	26		
James Madison	VA			36
Henry Marchant	RI		40	
John Mathews	SC		37	
James McHenry	MD			34
Thomas McKean	DE	46	51	
Arthur Middleton	SC	34		
Thomas Mifflin	PA			43
Gouverneur Morris[3]	PA		29[1]	35
Lewis Morris	NY	50		
Robert Morris	PA	42	47	53
John Morton	PA	52		
Thomas Nelson	VA	37		
William Paca	MD	35		

NAME		1776 Dec	1781 Conf	1787 Const
Robert Treat Paine	MA	45		
William Paterson	NJ			42
John Penn	NC	36	41	
Charles C. Pinckney	SC			41
Charles Pinckney	SC			30
George Read	DE	43		54
Joseph Reed	PA		40	
Daniel Roberdeau	PA		54	
Caesar Rodney	DE	47		
George Ross	PA	46		
Benjamin Rush	PA	30		
Edward Rutledge	SC	26[1]		
John Rutledge	SC			48
Nathaniel Scudder	NJ		48	
Roger Sherman	CT	55	60	66
James Smith	PA	57		
Jonathan B. Smith	PA		39	
Richard D. Spaight	NC			29
Richard Stockton	NJ	45		
Thomas Stone	MD	33		
George Taylor	PA	60		
Edward Telfair	GA		46	
Matthew Thornton	NH	62		
Nicholas Van Dyke	DE		43	
George Walton	GA	35		
John Walton	GA		43	
George Washington	VA			55
John Wentworth	NH		36	
William Whipple	NH	46		
John Williams	NC		50	
William Williams	CT	45		
Hugh Williamson	NC			52

NAME		1776 Dec	1781 Conf	1787 Const
James Wilson	PA	33		44
John Witherspoon	NJ	53	58	
Oliver Wolcott	CT	49	54	
George Wythe	VA	50		X[4]
TOTALS		56	48	39

[1]youngest signer
[2]oldest signer

[3]Morris represented Pennsylvania, to where he had moved from New York, at the Constitutional Convention.

[4] "X" = Delegate George Wythe (VA), signer of the Declaration, did not sign the Constitution (He favored acceptance but was absent on the day of signing.)

[4] "X" = Delegate Elbridge Gerry (MA), signer of the Declaration and Articles of Confederation, did not sign the Constitution. (He was opposed.)

2. **THE CONSTITUTIONAL CONVENTION DELEGATES**:

55 delegates participated in the Constitutional Convention.

30 of the 55 delegates served in the Revolutionary War.

42 of the delegates served in the Continental Congress.

41 delegates of the 55 participants attended the final session of the Convention.

<u>4 Delegates did not attend the final session, did not sign the Constitution, and were thought to be opposed</u>:

John Lansing, Jr. (NY); Luther Martin (MD); John Francis Mercer (MD); Robert Yates (NY).

<u>9 Delegates did not attend the final session, did not sign the Constitution, but were thought to be in favor</u>:

William Richardson Davie (NC); Oliver Ellsworth, (CT); William Houstoun (GA); William Churchill Houstoun (NJ); Alexander Martin (NC); James McClurg (VA); William Pierce (GA); Caleb Strong (MA); George Wythe (VA). Delegate John Dickinson (DE) did not attend but gave written instructions to George Read (DE) to sign on his behalf.

Delegates John Pickering and Benjamin West were appointed by the New Hampshire legislature, but never attended because the New Hampshire legislature refused to pay their expenses.

Rhode Island boycotted and sent no delegates to the Constitutional Convention.

<u>39</u> delegates signed the document.

38 delegates in attendance signed. John Dickinson did not attend but had George Read sign for him. 3 delegates in attendance on the last day chose not to sign: Elbridge Gerry (MA); George Mason (VA); Edmund Randolph (VA).

3. **NOTES REGARDING THE SIGNERS OF OUR FOUNDING DOCUMENTS**:

- All of the signers of the Declaration of Independence were members of the Continental Congress at the time of their signing. (The Declaration was a product of that Congress.)

- All of the signers of the Articles of Confederation were also members of the Continental Congress at the time. (The Articles of Confederation was a product of that Congress.)

- Most of the delegates to the Constitutional Convention were *not* members of the Confederation Congress. The Convention was authorized and charged by the Congress, with the expectation that their work would be reported back to them for action.

- 2 people signed all three of our key founding documents: Robert Morris (PA) and Roger Sherman (CT).

- 4 people signed the Articles of Confederation and the Constitution: Morris and Sherman, plus Daniel Carroll (MD), and John Dickinson (DE).

- 6 people signed the Declaration of Independence and the Constitution: Morris and Sherman, plus George Clymer (PA), Benjamin Franklin (PA), George Read (DE), James Wilson (PA).

- 16 Founders signed both the Declaration of Independence and the Articles of Confederation.

Presidents of the Congress under the Articles of Confederation: John Hanson (MD) was elected "our first President" in 1781. He was followed subsequently by Elias Boudinot (NJ), Thomas Mifflin (PA), Richard Henry Lee (VA), John Hancock (MA, who had already served once before when the Declaration of Independence was adopted before the subsequent adoption of the

Articles), Nathaniel Gorham (MA), Arthur St. Clair (PA), and Cyrus Griffen (VA). No individual could serve as president more than one year within any three year period.

APPENDIX 2:

<u>FOOTNOTES</u>

DEDICATION
[1] The "anonymous" quote in the Dedication is from a family history compilation for the Allen family.

II. INTRODUCTION
[1] "Common Sense," Thomas Paine, Barnes & Noble Classics, 978-1-59308-209-3, pg 13
[2] "First Prayer at Jamestown," www.crossroads.to
[3] "God Is Red," Vine Deloria, Jr, 978-1-55591-498-1, pg 51

IV. THE SECOND CONTINENTAL CONGRESS
[1] "1776," by David McCollough, 0-7432-2671-2, page 113.
[2] "Common Sense," Thomas Paine, Barnes & Noble Classics, 978-1-59308-209-3, pg 31
[3] Ibid, pg 63
[4] Ibid, pg 18
[5] Ibid, pg 17
[6] Ibid, pg 64
[7] Ibid, pg 385
[8] Ibid, pg 381
[9] "The Essential Wisdom of the Founding Fathers," Carol Kelly-Gangi, 978-1-4351-1149-3, page 31
[10] "Signing Their Lives Away," Denise Kiernan & Joseph D'Agnese, 978-1-59474-330-6, page 104.
[11] "The Essential Wisdom of the Founding Fathers," Carol Kelly-Gangi, 978-1-4351-1149-3, page 17
[12] "The Writings of George Washington," volume 26, John C. Fitzpatrick, editor, page 104.

V. THE CONFEDERATION CONGRESS
[1] "The Articles of Confederation," www.barefootsworld.net/aoc1777.html

VI. THE CONSTITUTIONAL CONVENTION

[1] "Plain, Honest Men, The Making of the American Constitution," Richard Beeman, 978-1-4000-6570-7, page 83
[2] Ibid, page 159

VII. THE DIVIDING ISSUES
[1] "Plain, Honest Men, The Making of the American Constitution," Richard Beeman, 978-1-4000-6570-7, page 114
[2] Ibid, page 231
[3] Ibid, page 280
[4] Ibid, page 280
[5] Ibid, page 279
[6] Ibid, page 279
[7] Ibid, page 302
[8] Ibid, page 248
[9] Ibid, page 299
[10] Ibid, page 238
[11] Ibid, page 238
[12] Ibid, page 215

VIII. CONCLUDING THE CONVENTION
[1] "Plain, Honest Men, The Making of the American Constitution," Richard Beeman, 978-1-4000-6570-7, page 357
[2] Ibid, page 270
[3] Ibid, page 360-361
[4] "Miracle at Philadelphia," Catherine Drinker Brown, 978-0-316-10398-5, page 263
[5] "Plain, Honest Men, The Making of the American Constitution," Richard Beeman, 978-1-4000-6570-7, page 367
[6] Ibid, page 412
[7] "Journal of the Federal Convention Kept by James Madison," James Madison, edited by E.H. Scott,
        978-1-58477-256-9, pg 51

IX. ACCEPTANCE BY THE PEOPLE – JUST BARELY
[1] Ibid, page 245
[2] Ibid, page 372
[3] Ibid, page 381
[4] Ibid, page ?????
[5] Ibid, page 390
[6] Ibid, page 396
[7] Ibid, page 397
[8] Ibid, page 400

X. UNFINISHED BUSINESS: THE BILL OF RIGHTS
[1] Ibid, page 342
[2] "Miracle at Philadelphia," Catherine Drinker Brown, 978-0-316-10398-5, page 245
[3] "Plain, Honest Men, The Making of the American Constitution," Richard Beeman, 978-1-4000-6570-7, page 343
[4] The Essential Wisdom of the Founding Fathers, Carol Kelly-Gangi, 978-1-4351-1149-3, page 48

XI. ACCOMPLISHMENT AND EXPECTATION
[1] "The Essential Wisdom of the Founding Fathers," Carol Kelly-Gangi, 978-1-4351-1149-3, page 37

XII. THE TRUTHS OF THE CONSTITUTIONAL AGREEMENT
[1] "The Essential Wisdom of the Founding Fathers," Carol Kelly-Gangi, 978-1-4351-1149-3, page 33
[2] "Plain, Honest Men, The Making of the American Constitution," Richard Beeman, 978-1-4000-6570-7, page 183
[3] "The Essential Wisdom of the Founding Fathers," Carol Kelly-Gangi, 978-1-4351-1149-3, page 39
[4] Ibid, page 40
[5] Ibid, page 66
[6] "Plain, Honest Men, The Making of the American Constitution," Richard Beeman, 978-1-4000-6570-7, page 270
[7] Ibid, page 270
[8] "The Essential Wisdom of the Founding Fathers," Carol Kelly-Gangi, 978-1-4351-1149-3, page 47
[9] Wall panel at Jefferson Memorial
[10] "The Essential Wisdom of the Founding Fathers," Carol Kelly-Gangi, 978-1-4351-1149-3, page 42
[11] Ibid, page 70
[12] Ibid, page 46
[13] Ibid, page 61
[14] Ibid, page 63
[15] Ibid, page 43
[16] Ibid, page 43
[17] Ibid, page 62
[18] Ibid, page 61
[19] Ibid, page 62
[20] Ibid, page 62
[21] Ibid, page 49
[22] Ibid, page 49
[23] Ibid, page 48

[24] Ibid, page 60
[25] Ibid, page 37
[26] Ibid, page 13
[27] Ibid, page 64
[28] Ibid, page 27
[29] Ibid, page 33
[30] "Plain, Honest Men, The Making of the American Constitution," Richard Beeman, 978-1-4000-6570-7, page 179
[31] Ibid, page 179
[32] "The Essential Wisdom of the Founding Fathers," Carol Kelly-Gangi, 978-1-4351-1149-3, page 73
[33] "Plain, Honest Men, The Making of the American Constitution," Richard Beeman, 978-1-4000-6570-7, page 177
[34] Ibid, page 181

XIII. RELIGION AND THE FOUNDING OF AMERICA

[1] "Religious Affiliation of the Founding Fathers," Adherents.com
[2] "The Faiths of the Founding Fathers," David L. Holmes, 0-19-530092-0, page 46
[3] "Deism," Wikipedia
[4] "The Faiths of the Founding Fathers," David L. Holmes, 0-19-530092-0, page 55
[5] Ibid, page 64
[6] Ibid, page 71
[7] Ibid, page 78
[8] Ibid, page 78
[9] "The Essential Wisdom of the Founding Fathers," Carol Kelly-Gangi, 978-1-4351-1149-3, page 31
[10] Ibid, page 31
[11] Ibid, page 44
[12] Ibid, page 77
[13] Ibid, page 64
[14] Ibid, page 67
[15] Ibid, page 75
[16] Ibid, page 51
[17] Ibid, page 73
[18] 1822 letter to Dr. Benjamin Waterhouse
[19] "The Essential Wisdom of the Founding Fathers," Carol Kelly-Gangi, 978-1-4351-1149-3, page 74
[20] Letter to Henry Fry, The Jefferson Bible, page 77
[21] 1816 letter to Mrs. Samuel H. Smith
[22] "The Essential Wisdom of the Founding Fathers," Carol Kelly-Gangi, 978-1-4351-1149-3, page 75

[23] Wall panel at Jefferson Memorial: Religious Freedom
[24] 1816 letter to Mrs. Samuel H. Smith
[25] "Lee," Douglas Southall Freeman, Richard Harwell, adapter, 978-0-684-82953-1, page 93

XV. FINAL WORDS FROM OUR FOUNDING FATHERS

[1] "The Essential Wisdom of the Founding Fathers," Carol Kelly-Gangi, 978-1-4351-1149-3, page 33
[2] Ibid, page 37
[3] Ibid, page 34
[4] "Daniel of Saint James Jenifer," Wikipedia,
[5] "The Essential Wisdom of the Founding Fathers," Carol Kelly-Gangi, 978-1-4351-1149-3, page 38
[6] Ibid, page 94
[7] Ibid, page 95

APPENDIX 3:

REFERENCE SOURCES & RECOMMENDED READINGS

Journal of the Federal Convention, Kept by James Madison
James Madison; E. H. Scott, editor; The Lawbook
Exchange, Ltd.; 978-1-58477-256-9

Plain, Honest Men; The Making of the American Constitution
Richard Beeman, Random House, New York   ISBN:
978-1-4000-6570-7

Miracle at Philadelphia;
The Story of the Constitutional Convention May to September 1787
Catherine Drinker Bowen, Little Brown and Company
ISBN: 978-0-316-10398-5

1776
David McCollough, Simon and Schuster
ISBN: 0-7432-2671-2

The Essential Wisdom of the Founding Fathers
Edited by Carol Kelly-Gangi, Fall River Press
ISBN: 978-1-4351-1149-3

The Faiths of the Founding Fathers
David L. Holmes, Oxford University Press
ISBN: 0-19-530092-0

Common Sense and Other Writings
  Thomas Paine, Introduction & Notes by Joyce Appleby,
  Barnes and Noble Classics
    ISBN: 978-1-59308-209-3

Signing Their Lives Away;
The Fame and Misfortune of the Men Who Signed the Declaration
of Independence
  Denise Kiernan and Joseph D'Agnese, Quirk Books
    ISBN: 978-1-59474-330-6

The Federalist (Papers)
  Various editions available.

A People's History of the United States; 1492 to Present
  Howard Zinn, Harper's Perennial
    ISBN: 978-0-06083-865-2

14. AUTHOR AND PUBLICATIONS

Randy Bell lives in the mountains of western North Carolina. He is a life-long student of spirituality as well as American history who spent 30 years in higher education as a teacher, administrator, and independent management consultant to colleges and universities across the United States. He is currently the founder and Director of Spring Creek Spirituality for spiritual training, has written eleven books, and writes two blogs on a variety of spiritual and social commentary topics. He is a member of the North Carolina Writer's Network and Spiritual Directors International.

Other publications by Randy Bell available from
www.McKeeLearningFoundation.com

Books:
God and Me: A Statement of Belief
    ISBN-13: 978-0-9710549-5-0

Lessons from the Teacher Jesus
    ISBN-13: 978-0-9710549-2-9

Lessons from the Teacher Buddha
    ISBN-13: 978-0-9710549-7-4

Lessons from the Teacher Moses
    ISBN-13: 978-0-9710549-8-1

Lessons from the Teacher Muhammad
    ISBN-13: 978-0-9710549-9-8

Buddhism: An Introductory Guide
ISBN-13: 978-0-9710549-1-2

Starting A Personal Meditation Practice
ISBN-13: 978-0-9895428-0-7

Unpacking The Boxes Of Our Attachments
ISBN-13: 978-0-9895428-1-4

*Forms of Meditation: Methods and Practices
for Contemplation and Prayer*
ISBN-13: 978-0-9710549-6-7

The Seven Virtues of a Spiritual Life
ISBN-13: none

Career Choices For Your Soul
ISBN-13: 978-0-9710549-4-3

Executive's Guidebook for Institutional Change
ISBN: 0-9710549-0-8

<u>Blog Commentaries</u>:

<u>Thoughts From The Mountain</u>
www.ThoughtsFromTheMountain.blogspot.com

A social commentary from a spiritual and ethical perspective.

<u>Our Spiritual Way</u>
www.OurSpiritualWay.blogspot.com

*Supporting personal commitment, individual insight,
and listening to guidance
as we share our spiritual journeys together.*

www.ingramcontent.com/pod-product-compliance
Lightning Source LLC
Chambersburg PA
CBHW022132080426
42734CB00006B/327